amy willcock's
aga baking

amy willcock's aga baking

TED SMART

For Harriet and Charlotte, Mummy's little helpers!

Author's acknowledgments
I am indebted to many people who have helped me with this book and in particular for their recipes,
support and critiques! Huge thanks to Grace Cheetham and the Ebury team; Sarah Wooldridge and
Lucy Hutton at IMG; my recipe testers Laurence Coates, Anthony Audette and Anthony Athekame;
Kevin Mangeolles and all at The George; recipe givers Janice Voyce and Sue McGeoch; Catherine
and Jo who keep the home fires burning; Ray and Jim for eating all the endless cakes; and last but
not least my family, Jeremy, Harriet and Charlotte. Thank you!

First published in Great Britain in 2003

This edition produced for The Book People Ltd, Hall Wood Avenue, Haydock, St Helens WA11 9UL

1 3 5 7 9 10 8 6 4 2

Text © Amy Willcock 2003
Photographs © William Lingwood 2003

First published by Ebury Press
Random House, 20 Vauxhall Bridge Road, London SW1V 2SA

Random House Australia (Pty) Limited
20 Alfred Street, Milsons Point, Sydney, New South Wales 2061, Australia

Random House New Zealand Limited
18 Poland Road, Glenfield, Auckland 10, New Zealand

Random House South Africa (Pty) Limited
Endulini, 5A Jubilee Road, Parktown 2193, South Africa

The Random House Group Limited Reg. No. 954009

www.randomhouse.co.uk

A CIP catalogue record for this book is available from the British Library.

Editor: Gillian Haslam
Designer: Christine Wood
Photographer: William Lingwood
Props stylist: Tessa Evelegh
Food stylist: Jenny White
Illustrations: Hannah Popham

ISBN 0 09189182 5

Papers used by Ebury Press are natural, recyclable products made from wood grown in
sustainable forests.

Printed and bound in Singapore by Tien Wah Press

contents

Introduction

Baking is a science. Everything must be weighed and measured accurately and tins must be of the right size. For the most part, there is a lot of flexibility when cooking non-baking recipes. Measurements don't have to be quite so precise and, at the end of the day, very few legs of lamb sink in the middle!

Keeping an audience's attention at a cookery demonstration can be challenging after the first hour and a half. After lunch it is almost impossible – the combination of a delicious lunch, new-found friends and a glass of wine means all you want to do is curl up and have a snooze. That's why I always do the baking section of my Aga workshops after lunch because I know it is a sure winner for keeping people's attention. Everyone wants to know the secret of baking in an Aga.

As with all Aga cooking, the trick is to cook by oven position and time. It doesn't matter if you have a 2- or 4-oven Aga – wonderful baking results can be achieved if you simply adjust your baking skills. Never having to pre-heat an oven means that whipping up a little chocolate cake is as easy as pie and don't even contemplate buying a bread-making machine – the Aga Roasting Oven is the best domestic oven on the market today to compare with a commercial baker's oven. With an Aga, fresh hot bread can be a reality every morning!

This book includes both old classics and new favourites. There is simply no other oven that cooks a fruit cake as well as an Aga Simmering Oven (see page 20) and the Roasting and Baking Ovens in an Aga are ideal for recipes such as chocolate-dipped pecan shortbread squares (see page 115) and peanut butter cupcakes (see page 155).

My aim with this book is to help you to get the best baking results out of your Aga. Most modern cooks will happily try a new meat or vegetable recipe but are terrified if the words 'baking' or 'cake' appear. For the first-time Aga baker, it can be nerve-racking as there are no dials to adjust to specific temperatures and some cakes can take a very long time indeed to cook. Baking hints and tips appear throughout the book, as well as answers to the most common baking queries and information on the best raw ingredients to buy (at home I try to be as organic as possible). I truly believe that by cooking and baking with an Aga regularly, Aga cooks become intuitive cooks and really have a feel for the dishes they are creating.

You may remember your grandmother's light touch with an apple pie, but will your grandchildren? This book will make sure they do.

Baking with an Aga

The first thing you need to understand about all Aga cookery is that baking and cooking is done by oven position and time. When it comes to baking, this fact can seem terrifying as all conventional recipes are written using temperature and time, which is not at all helpful to the Aga cook. If you find that the oven or hotplate I specify in my recipes gives out too much or too little heat, simply move the dishes around until you get it right. The advantage of baking in an Aga is that there is no waiting – the ovens need no pre-heating, therefore giving you an instant reason to whip up a cake or a home-made calzone.

With most recipes you can get away with adding and substituting ingredients, but baking is more scientific and if you start improvising too much you may find the recipes don't work. Measurements need to be specific and there is no use fighting the fact that metric is here to stay. Invest in a good set of scales and a decent measuring jug and working in metric will no longer seem so daunting.

Nowadays I seem to meet more and more people with wheat intolerance, some because it's a fashion and some due to serious health allergies. For this reason I have included some wheat-free recipes in the book. Not all the wheat-free flours can be substituted for regular flour and you may have to play around with them until you match the right flour to the right recipe. My favourite to use as a general all-purpose flour is rice flour.

AGA BAKING KNOW-HOW

Whether your Aga is new or old, no two Aga cookers are alike. Knowing the ins and outs of your Aga will be a huge advantage when it comes to baking. The unique Aga burner heats all Aga cookers in the same way, regardless of the type of fuel – electric, gas or oil. A thermostat automatically controls all Aga cookers and each part of the Aga is pre-set to different heats. The heat indicator (see page 17) should be consulted first thing in the morning to make sure all is well and the Aga is up to temperature. The mercury should sit as close as possible to the black line, which means that the correct amount of heat is stored and your Aga is fully up to heat.

The ovens on the right-hand side of the cooker are externally vented which is why there is no transfer of smells from foods cooked in the same oven (e.g. you can bake a cake and cook fish in the same oven at the same time and they will not be tainted) and this also keeps cooking smells out of the kitchen.

For the Aga to be at its most efficient, remember three important things:

- Cook as much as possible in the ovens.
- Keep the lids down.
- Use the correct cookware for each recipe and make sure cookware bottoms are clean, flat and crumb-free.

AGA OVENS

If you have a 4-oven Aga you will have a built-in Baking Oven and the majority of your baking will be done here. It sits at about 180–200°C/350–400°F – just the right temperature for most baking. If, however, you have a 2-oven Aga, you will need to invest in a few extra bits of equipment – the Aga Cake Baker (for cakes that require more than 40 minutes baking) and two or three Cold Plain Shelves, which turn the Roasting Oven into a moderate oven ideal for baking.

Really knowing your individual Aga and how it behaves is essential for good Aga baking skills. The Aga cooker's radiant heat means that valuable moisture is locked into food and opening the oven door and looking at the food is not a problem – the cast-iron ovens contain the all-round heat, allowing you to open the oven door as often as necessary.

THE BOILING PLATE

The Boiling Plate is the hottest plate as it is above the burner unit. Use it for bringing saucepans to the boil as well as any recipe that requires a high heat. Put the kettle on to the Boiling Plate and use this plate to make toast using the Aga Toaster.

THE SIMMERING PLATE

The Simmering Plate is just that – the perfect plate to use when you require a gentle heat. The greatest use of the Simmering Plate is as an instant griddle – it's fantastic for pancakes. I cook directly on the plate using Bake-O-Glide (see page 12) almost every day. As well as being easy to use and clean, no fat is required so low-fat cooking couldn't be simpler. If you don't possess Bake-O-Glide (and shame on you if you don't!), you can cook on the metal surface but you will need to season it like a frying pan and wipe small amounts of oil across the surface on a piece of kitchen paper.

Remember the 80/20 split – 80% of cooking to be done in the ovens and 20% of cooking to be done on the plates. Keep the lids down as much as possible to conserve heat.

THE WARMING PLATE (4-OVEN AGA ONLY)

Use the Warming Plate to keep dishes warm and for melting ingredients like butter and chocolate.

THE ROASTING OVEN

The hottest oven is the Roasting Oven. It has four cooking areas:

High – top of the oven – first/second set of runners

Middle – centre of the oven – third set of runners

Low – near the bottom – fourth set of runners

Floor – directly on the oven floor

The left-hand side of the oven near the burner unit is usually slightly hotter.

2-oven Aga

Roasting Oven – top right

Simmering Oven – bottom right

4-oven Aga

Roasting Oven – top right

Baking Oven – bottom right

Simmering Oven – top left (there is only one runner in the 4-oven Aga Simmering Oven)

Warming Oven – bottom left

The runners inside the ovens are always counted from top to bottom.

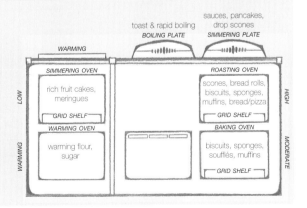

What cooks where

High – Top of the oven

Perfect for browning scones, popovers and the tops of puddings like lemon meringue pie.

Middle – Centre of the oven

2-oven Aga owners will use this area the most for general baking. By sliding in the Cold Plain Shelf, this oven becomes a moderate oven. Crumbles, muffins and cookies can all be baked here.

Low – Bottom of the oven

Sponge cakes are cooked on a grid shelf placed on the floor of the oven with the Cold Plain Shelf on the set of runners just above so that the heat is reduced to make a moderate oven. When making sponge cakes do not use the cake baker; instead use heavy-based tins (see page 11).

Floor

It has been said that this is the nearest a domestic oven can get to a professional baker's oven. I bake bread directly on the floor of this oven with fantastic results. An essential piece of equipment is my Oven Reach (see page 12), which is perfect for retrieving freshly baked loaves from the Roasting Oven floor. This is also where pastry tarts and pies are cooked.

THE BAKING OVEN

This is the oven for home baking. It tends to be slightly hotter towards the top.

What cooks where

Top of the oven

Genoise sponges and fairy cakes are best baked in this area.

Centre

Sponge cakes, muffins, cookies and crumbles are baked here.

Bottom

Cook soufflés and cheesecakes on a grid shelf on the floor of the oven.

THE SIMMERING OVEN

This is the most versatile and remarkable oven of the Aga. Nothing bakes a better fruit cake than the Aga Simmering Oven. Milk-based puddings, custards and meringues couldn't be simpler. Almost everything except meringues are started somewhere else. If you are a 2-oven Aga owner, this is where cheesecakes can be baked without fear of cracking. If you thought this was just a place to keep food ticking over, you will have been under-utilising a large part of your Aga.

What cooks where

Centre

Rice puddings, baked custards, steamed puddings and crumbles will all be started either in the Roasting Oven or on the Boiling Plate, then transferred to the Simmering Oven for long, slow, gentle baking.

Bottom

Place fruit cakes and meringues near the bottom of the oven for terrific results.

Floor

Slide the grid shelf on to the floor of the Simmering Oven to finish baking cheesecakes. For 2-oven Aga owners, use the Simmering Oven to dry fruit.

THE WARMING OVEN (4-OVEN AGA ONLY)

Just what it says it is! If you have one, use it for drying herbs and warming ingredients as well as keeping food and sauces warm.

The Aga Cake Baker

Using the Cake Baker means there is no need to turn cakes and no fear of over-browning. To use the Cake Baker, select the correct size of tin for your cake and remove the trivet from inside the Cake Baker. Put the Cake Baker with the lid on to the floor of the Roasting Oven to heat up. Pour your cake mix into the tin and remove the Cake Baker from the oven. Carefully set the trivet and cake tin inside the Cake Baker. Replace the lid, put the Cake Baker on the Roasting Oven floor and set your timer.

THE 3-OVEN AGA

In 2003 Aga launched its new 3-oven Aga – the GC3 model. It is basically a 2-oven Aga with a Baking Oven. The ovens are as follows:

Roasting Oven – top right

Simmering Oven – bottom right

Baking Oven – bottom left

Control Panel – top left

At the time of going to print, this new Aga is only available for use with LPG and natural gas with a conventional flue.

BAKEWARE FOR YOUR AGA

All newly purchased Aga cookers come with the following basic Aga kit:

   2 grid shelves

   1 large roasting tin and grill rack

   1 half-size roasting tin and grill rack

   1 Cold Plain Shelf

   1 Aga Toaster

   1 wire brush

A lot of people assume that you cannot bake a cake successfully in an Aga – well, that is just not true and this book proves it. What is absolutely paramount to good baking is good equipment. Scales must be accurate and tins must be warp-proof and heavy, especially cake tins. If someone comes to me with a particular problem with a cake recipe, I always ask them to bring in the tin so I can see it and, believe me, most should have seen a dustbin years ago. Invest in good bakeware and it will save you time, money and your cakes!

I have recently launched my own 'Rangeware' cookware specially designed for use with Aga cookers (see page 160). The baking trays fit directly on to the runners and all of my range can be used anywhere in or on the Aga. I hold a very strong belief that if cookware can't go in all the ovens, then it's really not worth buying. As I am a cookshop addict, I always look out for bakeware wherever I travel, to the extent that my suitcase always has far more pots and pans in it than clothes!

Overleaf you will find a list of what I consider essential equipment for baking. I recommend that the tins should all be hard anodised items. You may find that darker coloured tins need a shorter cooking time than lighter ones, such as aluminium, because dark colours absorb heat more quickly.

It is vital that you use the correct size of tin for cakes or you will have baking disasters. Most of the recipes in this book call for 20.5 cm tins. Cooking times and oven positions are calculated according to the size of tin specified.

2 x half-size shallow baking trays 34.5 x 23.5 cm

1 x large shallow baking tray 46 x 34.5 cm

1 x 20.5 cm round cake tin, loose base

2 x 20.5 cm sponge tins, loose base

2 x 18 cm sponge tins, loose base

1 x 20.5 cm square cake tin, loose base

1 x 27 cm Tarte Tatin dish

1 x 25.5 cm shallow round tart tin, loose base

1 x half-size traybake 34.5 x 24 x 4 cm

1 x full-size traybake 46 x 34.5 x 4 cm

1 x 12-hole muffin tin

2 x loaf tins (either 900 g or 450 g size)

1 x Aga Cake Baker (for 2-oven Aga owners)

1 Oven Reach

3 Cold Plain Shelves

2 grid shelves

For large cakes you can use the large- and half-size roasting tins.

Oven Reach

Bake-O-Glide

No kitchen can be considered complete without this wondrous cooking paper. I use it all the time and everywhere. It can even be washed in the dishwasher! You can use it directly on the Simmering Plate for cooking recipes like pancakes. I always line the bottom of cake tins with it and also use it on the floor of the Roasting Oven when baking bread. I strongly urge you to buy Bake-O-Glide – it will be one of the best investments you make.

Weighing and measuring

Accuracy is key to baking. Invest in a good set of weighing scales. I like to use electronic scales (and keep a spare set of batteries in the kitchen in case the power runs out just as I am weighing the flour). Another key ingredient is a good set of measuring spoons and a large glass measuring jug.

I make no apology for using only metric. I see no point in giving imperial measurements when you have to buy everything in metric – I hear people in supermarkets trying to work out measurements in metric all the time. I do, however, use teaspoons and tablespoons because to weigh out 5 g or 15 g of something would be a bore. You can buy these in sets and I urge you when baking not to be tempted to use any old spoon for these measurements but a proper set of measuring spoons. Unless stated otherwise, all measurements are level.

Mixers

I use my Kitchen Aid to make the majority of my cakes and breads. You will need a good strong mixer with whisk, paddle and dough hook attachments. I also sometimes use a food processor for pastry, but do be careful when using one as they are so fast that you can overmix.

You will also need a variety of hand whisks, spatulas and spoons for folding and scraping. A serrated palette knife is very useful too.

Bits and pieces

For pastry you will need a rolling pin – buy a long one without handles. A selection of cutters for biscuits and cookies, pure bristle pastry brushes, wire cooling racks, and decorating items such as piping bags, nozzles and colourings are also required. A good set of spacious glass or stainless steel mixing bowls is essential for maximum air incorporation.

When you have made your cakes you will need to put them on something to serve them – I know this sounds obvious, but do have a few cake plates in different sizes so that you can display your cakes and home-made goodies to their best advantage.

You will also need round and square airtight tins to store and transport your baked goods. Remember to put the cake on to the inverted lid and place the deep tin over it – this way you only have to lift off the lid rather than wrestle with the cake.

Pastry rolling tip

This trick-of-the-trade will save you time and mess. Cling film is a huge help when you want to cover and store dishes, but it is also great for rolling out pastry. Tear off a long sheet of cling film and place it on to a spacious flat surface. Pop your pastry ready for rolling on top, then cover with another piece of cling film and start to roll. You will be able to move your pastry around freely, it will not stick to the rolling pin and will peel off easily.

CHOOSING INGREDIENTS

Flour

Which flour should I use for which recipe? Basically there is a flour for every occasion so with the amount of choice now available on the supermarket shelves you can go wild, discovering new tastes and textures to add individuality to your baking. I use rice flour quite a lot in my baking and when cooking wheat-free dishes. Be brave and try something different – for the most part you can simply replace wheat flour with rice flour but you will have to experiment as it can affect the consistency of some recipes. Wherever possible, I prefer to use organic flours and I do mill some of my own grains. Look at Middle Eastern cookery books for recipes that use chickpea flour and sorghum flour to make flat breads.

Strong flour

This comes in white, brown and wholemeal. This type of flour has a high protein content, making it ideal for breads, rolls, pizza and puff pastry.

Plain flour

This comes in white, brown and wholemeal and is made from a variety of hard and soft wheat to make it into 'all-purpose' flour. Use it for pastry, pancake and Yorkshire pudding batters, sauces, fruit cakes and shortbread recipes.

Self-raising flour

This comes in white, brown and wholemeal to which a raising agent has been added. This is the flour to use for cakes, scones, puddings, shortcrust pastry, teabreads and biscuits. If a recipe calls for self-raising flour and you have none, use 2½ tsp baking powder to every 225 g flour.

Also try to keep a few supermarket bread mixes to which only water needs to be added as stand-bys in your kitchen storecupboard – with an Aga and a bread mix you can have a loaf of freshly baked bread in just 45 minutes!

Store flour in a cool, dry place. I use large glass jars and label the glass with a china marker. Never mix old flour with new; always wash and thoroughly dry the container before adding new flour. Under the right conditions, white and self-raising flours will keep for 6–9 months, and wholemeal and brown flours for 2–3 months. If you come across a creepy-crawly (the official name is psocid), throw away the flour and any other foods that are infested. Vacuum and wash all the containers, shelves and cupboards well, ensuring they are very dry before putting away new foods. Notify the supplier (if you know who it is) of the infestation.

Wheat-free baking

I have experimented with rice and potato flours in baking and pastry making and I am very satisfied with the results. The textures are different and sometimes the 'rise' isn't as great as it should be, but all in all if you can't eat wheat, my All-in-one Wheat-free Sponge cake is very good (see page 102). Do experiment with the different flours on the market.

Fats

Nothing tastes like butter! It is certainly my fat of choice when baking. Cakes made with butter also keep moist longer than cakes made with margarine and will produce a softer cake where sometimes margarine produces a crumblier, slightly drier cake. Remember the rule is that whatever fat you use for cake making, it must be very soft so a knife easily slides through it. It usually takes about 30 minutes to come up to room temperature if placed near the Aga. The margarines made especially for baking are extremely good and because they are ready to use, and if I am honest, you will find a tub in my fridge for times when I need to whip up a cake for school in a matter of minutes.

Sugar

I like to use unrefined golden caster sugar. For some cakes you may like to use soft brown sugar. Another great sweetener is organic honey; the measurements are the same as for caster sugar.

Eggs

Please use organic eggs. All recipes use large eggs. If you store them in the refrigerator, bring the eggs up to room temperature about an hour before you want to use them. The chief constituents of eggs that affect baking are fat and albumen and they are valuable as raising agents. Eggs should be at least two days old for cake baking and for meringues. If an egg is too fresh, the albumen cannot hold as much air. Duck eggs are especially suitable for baking as they are larger and contain more protein and fat.

Raising agents

Always check the use-by dates on your baking powder and throw it away if it is out of date as its raising powers more than likely will have disappeared. Baking powder is usually a mixture of bicarbonate of soda and cream of tartar. All spoon measurements are level.

Air is very important to cake making. Always sift your flour and raising agent from a great height to incorporate as much air as possible into your mixing bowl. When an acid and an alkali are mixed together and moisture is added, they effervesce and a gas is formed. When heated, the gas is given off with greater force and thus rising occurs. Add your raising agent to the dry ingredients just before mixing with the liquid. The gas is activated as soon as it touches the liquid so it is therefore important to bake the cake mix immediately.

Yeast

I specify fresh yeast in my recipes and always have it in the fridge. You can buy it at the bakery counter in supermarkets or at your local bakery if you have one. If you run out, you can use 'easy blend yeast', using one 7 g sachet to every 650 g of strong bread flour and following the manufacturer's instructions

Pre-weighed mixes

It may sound really daft but one of the hardest parts about baking and cooking in general is getting all the ingredients weighed out and measured. If you can take away that obstacle, you will find yourself baking a cake, making bread or baking cookies more frequently. I like to have bags of dry cake, cookie and bread ingredients made up in my larder with a recipe sheet in the bag so that I don't have to search my books or files.

These also become great home-made presents when accompanied by a hand-carved wooden spoon, a pretty linen tea towel or even a large cook's apron. Tie it all up with a lovely ribbon or present it in a beautiful basket. Any child or busy friend will enjoy receiving such a pressie – all they have to add is the wet ingredients and stir!

Frozen puff pastry

I must confess here that I have only made puff pastry a few times in my life. I used to feel guilty about this until I found out that some very good chefs buy in their puff pastry. I really do think it is unrealistic to make it these days as we can buy such good frozen puff pastry in shops and supermarkets. I know a number of you will disagree with me and always swear to make it yourself and I admire you for this, but for me it will be store bought!

Spice mixtures

When making fruit pies or crumbles, I tend to use the same spice mixtures. So to make things easier and quicker, I make up spice mixes in jars and label them 'Apple Pie', 'Pumpkin Pie', and so on. To suit your palette I will leave the precise amounts up to you. When it comes to making your pie, all you need to do is add a teaspoonful of the required mix. Experiment and you will find a combination that will be your signature. I always recommend that you grate nutmeg fresh every time you use it as it loses so much flavour when stored in powdered form. Try to find whole nutmegs with the mace still on them.

Apple Pie Spice
    Ground cinnamon
    Ground cloves
    Ground cardamom

Pumpkin Pie Spice
    Ground ginger
    Ground cinnamon
    Allspice
    Cloves

Cinnamon Sugar for Streusel Topping
    Unrefined golden caster sugar
    Cinnamon
Add a cinnamon stick and ground cinnamon to a jar of caster sugar.

Vanilla Sugar
    Vanilla pods
    Unrefined golden caster sugar
Whiz up whole vanilla pods in caster sugar and store in glass jars.

Home-made Vanilla Extract

   15–20 vanilla pods – the more the better

   1 bottle of vodka

Split about 8 vanilla pods and stuff them into a sealable jar, then add the rest of the pods – a mason jar is fine or use the vodka bottle. Top the jar up with vodka and shake, then leave to marinate for a minimum of 3 months. Shake the jar every few weeks or, as I do, whenever you remember! When you are ready to use the vanilla extract, burst the swollen pods and squeeze the small seeds back into the vanilla extract. Decant into smaller glass bottles to use as gifts or for easy storage. Don't throw away the pods – use them for vanilla sugar or keep them stuffed in the bottles.

CONVERTING RECIPES FOR AGA USE

Remember the 80/20 split when it comes to converting recipes (80% of cooking in the ovens and 20% on the plates). Use the diagram on page 9 to help you decide where best to bake your recipe. For 2-oven Aga owners, for cakes that require over 40 minutes cooking, you can use a Cake Baker or the 'Before the Cake Baker' method given on page 17.

It is a good idea to underestimate timings slightly – I usually set my timer for 10 minutes less than a conventional recipe states. You can always leave the dish in for a little longer if necessary. And of course the great advantage with an Aga is that you can open the oven doors and look inside without fear of the cake collapsing.

Take a tart recipe, for instance. The ingredients and method are exactly the same but the conventional recipe calls for an oven pre-heated to 180°C/350°F/gas 4 and a blind-baked pastry case. The cooking time for blind baking is 10–15 minutes with a further 35–40 minutes after the filling is poured in.

For a 2-oven Aga

There is no need to pre-heat the Aga as it is always ready to bake and it is also unnecessary to blind bake unfilled pastry cases as the whole tart (base and filling) bakes at the same time. Make the pastry and line the tin according to the recipe and add the filling. Slide the tart tin directly on to the floor of the Roasting Oven and slide the Cold Plain Shelf on to the third set of runners above. Bake the tart for 20–25 minutes or until the filling is just set.

For a 4-oven Aga

As above, but the Roasting Oven is the best place for baking a pastry-lined tin.

AGA TEMPERATURES

These represent typical centre-oven temperatures:

Roasting Oven – hot

   Approx. 240–260°C

   Approx. 475–500°F

   Gas 8–9

Baking Oven – moderate

   Approx. 180–200°C

   Approx. 350–400°F

   Gas 4–6

Simmering Oven – slow

   Approx. 135–150°C

   Approx. 200–300°F

   Gas 1

Warming Oven – warm

   Approx. 70–100°C

   Approx. 150–200°F

   Gas ¼

Mercury position

Mercury in black area: less heat is stored so baking will take longer, temperature too low.

Mercury in red area: more than required amount of heat stored, temperature too high.

Mercury right on the bold black line: spot on!

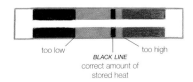

too low   BLACK LINE   too high
correct amount of
stored heat

the heat indicator

THE AGA WAY OF BAKING

Most people think that baking in an Aga is impossible but all you need to do is know your ovens, buy good quality bakeware and keep on checking! My party trick when I do a cookery demonstration is usually to bake an all-in-one sponge cake with the Roasting Oven door off. As I do the baking part of my demonstration in the afternoon, it ties in very nicely with the 'Cleaning your Aga' part. So, whilst I am showing the basic Aga cleaning methods, the cake is slowly baking. It is quite funny to see the audience's reaction when I remove the door – something you could never contemplate with a conventional cooker.

One of the many things I learned while testing recipes for this book is that many factors determine baking times, and some cakes take an inordinate amount of time to bake in an Aga. We used three different Aga cookers – one 4-oven and two 2-oven models – and I can tell you that sometimes a cake's timing can vary from as much as 1½ hours to 6 hours depending on the Aga. So much depends on how hot the ovens are when you start your cake. On average I found oil-fuelled Agas slightly slower than gas. In all honesty you must only use the timings as guidelines and check your food regularly when it is in the oven.

One golden Aga rule is, if it works for you carry on! Once you have recognised your cooker's hot spots and mastered its quirks, you will be the best judge of what works for you.

Bread baking tip

Buy a small cup-sized stainless steel beaker or mould. Fill it with cold water and put it in the Roasting Oven when baking bread. It will create the steam that is an essential ingredient in achieving a great bread crust. You can even splash water directly on to the Roasting Oven floor to create an instant burst of steam. This is good to do halfway through baking and just before the final 8 minutes of baking.

Before the Cake Baker

A really good baking tip for 2-oven Aga owners is to use the Cold Plain Shelf as a hot shelf. If you have a recipe that requires a longer cooking time, over 40 minutes or so, you will want to move the cake from the Roasting Oven to the Simmering Oven. The best way to continue the baking is to slide the Cold Plain Shelf (even if you don't need it) into the Roasting Oven to heat up so when you need to move your cake to the Simmering Oven, you move the shelf as well. Slide the now 'hot' Plain Shelf on to the desired runner, and continue baking the cake on it. The hot plain shelf gives an extra boost of heat to the cake and oven.

Cake testing

If a cake is done, the sides of the cake will be just coming away from the sides of the tin. Press the top of the cake lightly, if it is done it will spring back; if a little dent is left you need to give it a few more minutes in the oven.

Planning your baking

As it is better if the oven is a little cooler when you bake, try to plan your baking for the afternoon or after a major cooking session. Over the years I have picked up many useful tips from other Aga owners when it comes to baking. Some Aga owners swear by sliding a large roasting tray full of cold water into the Roasting Oven to cool the cooker down and then keep on changing it. Another tip is to boil the kettle and leave it on the Simmering Plate so that with the lid up the cooker will not be so hot. I prefer to plan my baking to follow a cooking session and I have lots of Cold Plain Shelves to keep me going.

It goes without saying that if you can make any of your dishes ahead of time, then do. Bread doughs can be made and proved for the first time then put in the fridge until you are ready to use them. Prepare as much as possible in advance so that all you are doing is opening an oven door and sliding something in. I always keep a few tart tins lined with sweet and savoury pastry in the freezer so that if I need a quick pudding or savoury tart when someone arrives unexpectedly, all I have to do is make up a filling and pop it into the oven. This is where we are so lucky – blind baking does not figure in an Aga owner's world!

AGA BAKING HINTS AND TIPS

● Plan to do your baking at a time when you know your Aga will be slightly cooler, such as after a large cooking session.

● Use heavy-based tins for all your baking and cake-making (see page 160 for suppliers).

● Use Bake-O-Glide to line cake tins.

● Use the Roasting Oven floor to bake bread.

● Use the Simmering Plate covered with a round piece of Bake-O-Glide to cook pancakes, drop scones and tuiles.

● Warm flour and sugar needed for recipes either at the back of the Aga or in the Simmering and Warming Ovens.

● Buy two Cold Plain Shelves – you can cool them down quickly by running them under cold water, but having an extra one will save this task.

● Use the black surface area of the top of the Aga to melt butter or chocolate for baking.

● Prove yeast-based recipes and bread dough next to the Aga – it can cut the proving time in half in some cases.

● Keep a kettle of boiling water going on the top of the Simmering Plate to lower an oven temperature.

● Invest in a good timer and a good set of scales – they will be your new best friends!

● Dry whisks, large baking sheets and awkward utensils at the back of the Aga top.

● Use the Cold Plain Shelf as a guide when you want to plan how best to use your oven space. Put the Cold Plain Shelf on to a work surface and arrange your saucepans/tins, etc. on top to see how much space you have.

● Refresh stale bread by spraying with water and baking it in the Roasting Oven for 5 minutes.

● For fast and easy food, use your Aga almost as you would a microwave – I know this sounds ridiculous but frozen foods do well in the Aga and when you want to heat something up in a hurry use one of the ovens. Frozen bread can be ready in just 10 minutes (but note that all defrosting should be done in a refrigerator).

● Wipe up spills immediately with a damp cloth and sweep away crumbs left on the hotplates and insides of the oven with the wire brush.

● Always have your Aga serviced by an approved Aga engineer. As a general rule, service it once a year for gas and electric and twice a year for oil.

Amy's biggest tip

Look at your dishes cooking and baking in the Aga frequently and don't be afraid to move the food around to another location in or on your Aga. If a hot plate is too hot, then move it. The recipe timings in this book are a guide, and remember that every Aga is different. Agas create intuitive cooks because of this. You will learn to cook by instinct.

AGA AT A GLANCE

Here are some general baking positions and timings.

Bread: Roasting Oven floor.

Cheesecake: grid shelf on the Roasting Oven floor with the Cold Plain Shelf above for 5–10 minutes, then move to the Simmering Oven for 35–45 minutes. You can start it in the Baking Oven for 15–20 minutes, then move to the Simmering Oven.

Cookies and biscuits: fourth set of runners in the Roasting Oven or third set of runners in the Baking Oven.

Frozen bread: fourth set of runners in the Roasting Oven or grid shelf on the floor of the Roasting Oven.

Frozen pastry cases: Roasting Oven floor.

Melting chocolate/butter: back of Aga on black enamel top, on the Warming Plate or in the Simmering Oven for 10 minutes.

Muffins: grid shelf on the floor of the Roasting Oven or fourth set of runners with the Cold Plain Shelf on the runners above; Baking Oven on third set of runners.

Pancakes: directly on the Simmering Plate surface using a piece of Bake-O-Glide or wipe a small amount of oil on to the surface.

Pizza: Roasting Oven floor for approximately 12 minutes.

Popovers: heat tin on the Roasting Oven floor, pour in batter, then move up to third set of runners.

Scones: third set of runners in the Roasting Oven.

Sponge cakes: grid shelf on the Roasting Oven floor with the the Cold Plain Shelf on the third set of runners.

A WORD ABOUT CAKES

For me, the discovery of what makes a great cake is purely a matter of science. As with all baking, exact measurements are necessary and a good consistent set of scales is a must.

The main ingredients for making cakes are flour, fat, sugar, eggs and a raising agent (baking powder). Fruit is also a staple in many recipes. In basic terms, when flour, which contains starch and a sticky substance called gluten, is combined with the other ingredients and heat is applied, the starch grains in the flour burst. The starch can then absorb and hold the moisture obtained from the sugar, butter and eggs or fruit. When moist, the gluten becomes firm. Moisture, when heated, turns into steam and the steam created blows out the gluten. More heat sets the gluten and holds it in an expanded condition – the 'risen' cake.

Cakes are classified according to the proportions fat, sugar and flour. Plain cakes have less fat to flour, while rich cakes have a high fat to flour ratio (the richness of the cake depends not so much on the proportion of fruit but of fat). Sponge cakes have a high proportion of air.

Cake tins must be strong, thick and solid. Thin tins are unsuitable for the Aga because the heat passes through more quickly than in a conventional oven and can therefore burn the outside of the cake while the middle is still uncooked. My range of cake tins is specially designed for Aga use (see page 160). I find that I don't need to grease my tins and only line the loose bottom with a pre-cut piece of Bake-O-Glide. If you are not sure how your tins will stand up, you may wish to line the sides with strips of Bake-O-Glide as well.

As with all Aga cooking and baking, recipes are cooked according to time and position, and there is no exception to this when baking cakes. The general rule regarding heat is the plainer the cake, the hotter the oven. If a cake has a large surface a hot oven is necessary; the heat can penetrate through to the inside and cook the ingredients more quickly without burning. This speed in cooking is an aid to successful baking. When a high instant heat is applied to a raising agent, it will give off a greater force of gas and the cake will rise much better. In rich cakes, the percentage of fat and sugar is higher than that of flour and there is a smaller proportion of gluten to hold the air and the gas from the raising agent should develop slowly. If an oven is too hot, it will burn the outside of the cake before the inside is cooked, therefore the richer the cake, the slower the oven. This is why the Simmering Oven is the perfect oven for baking fruit cakes.

Aga fruit cakes

Prepare your fruit cake recipe as usual, then place the tin on the third set of runners in the Simmering Oven. A 20.5 cm round fruit cake will take anywhere between 4 and 10 hours. The reason for the timing variation is that no two Aga cookers are the same. My own fruit cake recipe (see page 136) in the Simmering Oven takes about 6 hours.

Owners of 4-oven Agas may find that their Simmering Oven is slightly slower than a 2-oven Aga Simmering Oven. Start the cake off in the Baking Oven for 45–60 minutes, then transfer it to the Simmering Oven in as high a position as possible and cook for 4–10 hours, or longer in some cases. Another trick is to use the large grill rack from inside the large Roasting Tin. Put the grill rack directly on to the Simmering Oven floor and put the fruit cake directly on to it. If you feel you don't need the extra boost of the Baking Oven, bake the cake in the Simmering Oven only as above.

There is no need to line cake tins with brown paper or to cover with newspaper. Use Bake-O-Glide for ease of cake removal.

For 2-oven Aga owners, if you have an Aga Cake Baker you can use it for baking fruit cakes. It will reduce the baking time and still give a good result but you can't beat the Simmering Oven method.

COMMON REASONS FOR BAKING FAILURES

Fruit sunk to the bottom

It could be that the mixture was too moist. Fruit is heavy and it can sink before the starch cooks and the gluten sets. Fruit may fall to the bottom of the cake if it is added before the flour.

Heavy texture

The proportion of flour is too great or not enough air was beaten in – flour is heavy and tends to knock the air out so it must be folded very lightly. Beating and stirring the cake after flour is added must be avoided.

Cracked top

The cake has usually been baked in too hot an oven or it has been positioned too close to the top of the oven or the Plain Shelf. The top of the cake sets and therefore makes it very difficult for the gas to spread evenly around the cake.

Raised middle

The cake was put in too hot an oven, then moved to too low a temperature before the outside of the cake had a chance to set; or the mixture was not creamed enough.

Burnt bottom

The most obvious reason for a burnt cake bottom is too thin a tin (see page 11). The other problem that can occur is that not enough air circulates around the cake tin, as can be the case if you use the Plain Shelf instead of a grid rack. For fruit cakes and cakes requiring long baking times, start the cake off on the Grid Shelf then, when the cake is set, transfer it to a Hot Plain Shelf. To cool an oven and for extra absorption of heat in an oven, place a roasting tin containing either clean sand or water on the floor or the lower shelf.

Sunken centre

There are three reasons for this happening: too much raising agent, too hot an oven or – but this doesn't apply to Aga owners – slamming a conventional oven door soon after the cake has gone in, which lets in a sudden rush of cold air and changes the pressure in the oven, shaking the air out before the cake has a chance to set.

Spots on cake surface

The mixture wasn't creamed well enough so the sugar does not dissolve.

Swiss roll badly cracked

The oven was too cool. A Swiss roll needs to be baked quickly in a hot oven. The cake must be rolled on a damp cloth. Lay the rolling paper dusted with the sugar on top and turn the hot cake out and roll. When the hot cake is turned out on to it, steam accumulates and softens the outside of the roll, helping to prevent too much cracking.

**breakfast
and brunch**

panettone french toast

serves 6

4 eggs	**TO SERVE:**
50 ml milk	**unsalted butter**
1 tbsp Amaretto	**icing sugar**
generous grating of nutmeg	**honey**
6 slices panettone, each about 2 cm thick	

1 In a large flattish dish, combine the eggs, milk, Amaretto and nutmeg and beat well.

2 Place the large round piece of Bake-O-Glide on the SIMMERING PLATE.

3 Dip both sides of the panettone into the eggy mix. Spread a little butter over the Bake-O-Glide, place the eggy panettone on it and cook for a few minutes, then flip and continue cooking until both sides are golden.

4 Remove the panettone to a warm plate. Spread more butter on the bread, dust with icing sugar and drizzle over some honey. Serve either for breakfast or for pudding, or to accompany the Kashmir Plums (see page 122).

Conventional Baking:
Use a frying pan over a moderate heat.

standard white bread

makes 1 loaf

1 kg strong bread flour	**34 g fresh yeast**
27 g butter, softened	**600 ml warm water**
27 g salt	

1 Fit the dough hook on to an electric mixer and add the flour, butter and salt to the bowl. Mix to combine.

2 Crumble the yeast into 425 ml of the warm water and stir. When the yeast has melted, pour it into the flour. Add the rest of the water if the dough is too stiff. It is best to hold back a little water and add it if necessary rather than pour it all in and have to add more flour. Knead for 8 minutes on medium speed or until the dough is soft and elastic.

3 Lightly oil a bowl and place the dough in it. Cover with cling film and stand next to the Aga to double in size.

4 Punch the dough back, then mould into shape on a piece of Bake-O-Glide or place in a tin. Stand it near the Aga for 45–60 minutes or until it has risen.

5 Put the risen dough on to the floor of the ROASTING OVEN and place a stainless steel cup half-full of cold water next to it (the water will create steam). For extra steam, splash about 1 tbsp water directly on the floor of the oven towards the end of the baking time. Bake for 20–25 minutes or until the loaf sounds hollow when tapped on the underside. (If you are using Bake-O-Glide, put it on a shallow baking tray and slide the paper off the tray and on to the floor of the oven.) Remove from the tin and cool on a wire rack.

Conventional Baking:
Pre-heat the oven to 220ºC/425ºF/gas 7 and bake for 30–40 minutes in the centre of the oven.

right: panettone french toast

refrigerator white bread

This recipe appeared in my previous book, but I've included it again simply because it's such a useful recipe to have in your repertoire. The dough is prepared and refrigerated overnight, so all you have to do is bake it in the morning for fresh bread. Another great thing about this dough is that you can pull off small amounts to bake and leave the rest in the fridge for up to 2 days.

makes 1 loaf

1 kg strong white bread flour	**25 g salt**
25 g butter, softened	**35 g fresh yeast**
30 ml sunflower oil, plus more for greasing	**600 ml hand-hot water**

1 Fit the dough hook on to an electric mixer and add the flour, butter, oil and salt to the bowl. Mix to combine.
2 Crumble the yeast into 425 ml of the warm water and stir. When the yeast has melted, pour it into the flour. Add more of the warm water (to a maximum of 175 ml) if the dough is too stiff. It is best to hold back a little water and add it if necessary rather than pour it all in and have to add more flour. Knead for 8 minutes on medium speed or until the dough is soft and elastic.
3 Lightly oil a bowl and place the dough in it. Cover with cling film and refrigerate overnight.
4 When you are ready to bake the bread, remove the dough from the fridge and mould into shape on a piece of Bake-O-Glide or in a tin. Let it stand near the Aga for 45–60 minutes or until risen.
5 Bake on the floor of the ROASTING OVEN for 20–25 minutes or until it sounds hollow when tapped on the underside. (If using Bake-O-Glide, put it on a shallow baking tray, then slide the paper off the tray and on to the oven floor.) Cool on a wire rack.

Conventional Baking:
Pre-heat the oven to 220°C/425°F/gas 7 and bake for 30–40 minutes in the centre of the oven.

blackberry butter

Serve this at breakfast-time with brioche or at teatime with scones.

250 g unsalted butter, at room temperature	**150 g ripe blackberries**

1 Whizz the butter and fruit together in a food processor to form a smooth purée.

2 Spoon into a serving dish and refrigerate until 1 hour before serving.

chocolate bread

This recipe is best made using an electric mixer.

makes 1 large loaf

30 g unsalted butter, softened, plus extra for buttering the tins

85 g unrefined golden caster sugar, plus 2 tbsp for coating the tins

30 g fresh yeast

275 ml warm water

365 g strong bread flour

40 g good quality cocoa powder

1 tsp salt

oil, for greasing the bowl

50 g good quality dark chocolate, chopped into chunks

FOR THE GLAZE:

1 egg yolk

1 tbsp double cream

2 tbsp unrefined golden caster sugar

1 Butter the insides of a large loaf tin and coat with 2 tbsp golden caster sugar.

2 Put the yeast into a bowl, add half the water and stir.

3 Fit the dough hook on to the mixer and combine the flour, cocoa powder, sugar and yeast mix. Add the remaining water slowly – you made not need all of it or you may need a little more depending on the flour. Mix on a low speed for about 5 minutes. Turn off the machine and let the dough rest for 10–15 minutes.

4 Add the salt and butter to the dough and continue to knead with the machine on a medium speed for about 10 minutes or until the dough develops a shine.

5 Oil the inside of a large bowl. Turn out the dough, form into a ball and place inside the bowl. Cover with cling film and leave at the side of the Aga to rise.

6 When it has doubled in size, fold the chopped chocolate pieces into the dough, then lightly fold the dough into thirds (like an envelope), cover with cling film again and leave for 30 minutes.

7 Divide the dough into four equal pieces. Roll each piece into a ball and place all the balls in the prepared loaf tin. Cover with cling film and set near the Aga to double in size.

8 To prepare the glaze, mix the egg yolk and cream together. When the loaf is ready to be baked, brush very lightly with the glaze and sprinkle over the sugar.

9 Place the loaf tin on the floor of the ROASTING OVEN and bake for 20–25 minutes or until the bread sounds hollow when tapped on the underside (protect your hands when doing this).

10 Remove the tin to a wire rack and cool the bread in the tin for a few minutes before removing from the tin and cooling completely on the wire rack.

Conventional Baking:
Pre-heat the oven to 220ºC/425ºF/gas 7 and bake the bread as above.

oatmeal and cinnamon oven pancakes

serves 4–6

3 eggs	110 ml water
grating of fresh nutmeg	100 g oatmeal
1 tsp ground cinnamon	40 g clarified butter
175 g plain flour	icing sugar, for dusting
175 ml milk	maple syrup, to serve

1 Whisk the eggs, spices and flour together in a bowl and, still whisking, slowly add the milk and water. Stir in the oatmeal and set aside.

2 Put 1 tbsp clarified butter into a small cast iron frying pan (I use a 21 cm frying pan or my small tarte tatin dish) and heat it up in the ROASTING OVEN until it is smoking hot. Move the pan to the SIMMERING PLATE and pour in a ladleful of the batter.

3 Put the grid shelf on the third set of runners in the ROASTING OVEN and place the pan on it. Bake each pancake for 10–15 minutes or until it is risen and golden brown. Move the pancakes to a plate in the SIMMERING OVEN to keep warm and repeat until all the batter is used up.

4 Serve either straight away dusted with icing sugar and drizzled with maple syrup or, if cooked earlier in the day, re-heat for 8 minutes in the ROASTING OVEN before serving.

Conventional Baking:
Pre-heat the oven to 220ºC/425ºF/gas 7 and bake the pancakes as above.

baked eggs and bacon

serves 1

butter, at room temperature	1 egg
1 rasher of streaky bacon, fried and chopped into pieces	salt and pepper
	1 tbsp double cream

1 Butter the inside of a ramekin. Put the bacon pieces on the bottom of the ramekin.

2 Break the egg on top of the bacon and season with salt and pepper. Pour over the double cream and set the ramekin on a baking tray.

3 Slide the baking tray on to the third set of runners in the ROASTING OVEN and cook for 5–8 minutes.

4 Remove from the oven and place the ramekin on a dish. Serve accompanied by hot buttered toast cut into soldiers.

Conventional Baking:
Pre-heat the oven to 200ºC/400ºF/gas 6 and bake for 8–10 minutes.

right: oatmeal and cinnamon oven pancakes

brioche

makes 1 loaf

40 g fresh yeast	20 g salt
50 ml warm milk	700 g unsalted butter, softened
1 kg plain flour	
100 g unrefined golden caster sugar	FOR THE GLAZE:
12–15 eggs	1 egg yolk, beaten with 1 tbsp milk
700 ml water	

1 Crumble the yeast into the warm milk and mix until smooth. Put the flour and sugar into the bowl of an electric mixer with the dough hook attached and start the mixer on a slow speed. Pour in the yeast and milk and the water, then add the eggs one at a time. Next add the salt and butter and knead really well. It will appear very sloppy but persevere. When the dough comes away from the sides of the bowl it is ready.

2 Put the dough into a lightly greased large bowl and stand it to the side of the Aga for 1–2 hours or until it has doubled in size.

3 Knock back the dough and return it to the bowl. Chill in the fridge for a few hours.

4 Turn the dough out and shape it into a ball or plait or transfer to a tin. Leave to rise next to the Aga again until it has doubled in size, then glaze the top with the egg yolk mix.

5 Place the brioche on a grid shelf on the third set of runners in the ROASTING OVEN and bake for 40–45 minutes or until the brioche is golden and sonds hollow when tapped on the bottom. If you are using a tin, unmould immediately and cool on a wire rack.

Conventional Baking:
Pre-heat the oven to 200°C/400°F/gas 6 and bake for 40–45 minutes as above.

muffins

Muffins are fabulously versatile and the trick is not to over-work the batter. Use as few strokes as possible when mixing the ingredients. Don't worry if the mixture appears lumpy – the muffins will come out deliciously light after baking! To test if muffins are cooked in the middle, insert the point of a knife or a skewer. If it comes out clean, they are ready. If the mix is still loose, put them back in the oven for a few more minutes.

breakfast muffins

makes 12

250 g plain flour	1 vanilla pod, scraped of its seeds
150 g unrefined golden caster sugar	118 ml vegetable oil or melted butter
2 tsp baking powder	180 g fresh fruit such as blueberries, raspberries, chopped peaches, apricots, etc
pinch of salt	
1 large egg, slightly beaten	FOR THE TOPPING:
160 ml milk	200 g muesli

1 Line a muffin tin with muffin papers and set aside.

2 Mix together flour, sugar, baking powder and salt in a large bowl. Mix the egg, milk, vanilla seeds and oil or butter in another bowl. Make a well in the dry ingredients, add the fruit and pour in the wet ingredients. Using a large rubber spatula, fold the mix together using as few strokes as possible.

3 Spoon the mix into the muffin papers until they are half-full. Sprinkle over the muesli.

4 Put the grid shelf on to the floor of the ROASTING OVEN and silde in the muffin tin. Slide the COLD PLAIN SHELF on to the third set of runners and bake for 20–25 minutes or until golden. Remove from the tin and cool on a wire rack.

Conventional Baking:

Pre-heat the oven to 200ºC/400ºF/gas 6 and bake for 20–25 minutes as above.

courgette muffins

makes about 12

1 egg	½ tsp salt
85 ml honey	½ tsp freshly grated ginger
240 g courgettes, grated	1 tsp ground cinnamon
250 g plain flour (I sometimes use half plain flour and half wholewheat)	100 g chopped walnuts
½ tsp baking soda	80 g raisins
2 tsp baking powder	100 ml sunflower oil

1 Line a muffin tin with muffin papers and set aside.

2 Whisk together the egg, honey and courgettes in a bowl. Mix in the rest of the ingredients until just combined. Spoon the mix into the paper cases until they are half-full.

3 Bake the muffins on the third set of runners in the ROASTING OVEN for 20 minutes. For 4-oven Aga owners, bake on the third set of runners in the BAKING OVEN for 25 minutes. They are done when they are risen and lightly golden.

Conventional Baking:

Pre-heat the oven to 190ºC/375ºF/gas 5 and bake for 20–25 minutes.

healthy heavy muffins

This is more of a healthy eating muffin with a heavier texture.

makes 12

145 g wholewheat flour	2 tsp vanilla extract
75 g bran	160 ml honey
3 tbsp oatmeal	1 apple, grated
2 tsp baking powder	2 small carrots, peeled and grated
pinch of salt	160 ml apple purée
good grating of nutmeg	75 g dried figs, chopped
4 large eggs, slightly beaten	75 g chopped almonds
100 ml milk	zest of 1 organic orange

1 Line a muffin tin with muffin papers and set aside.

2 Mix together all the dry ingredients in a large bowl and all the wet in another bowl.

3 Make a well in the dry ingredients, add the fruit and nuts and pour in the wet ingredients. Using a large rubber spatula, fold the mix together using as few strokes as possible. Spoon the mix into the papers, filling them half-full if using a topping (see page 33) or to the top if not.

4 Put the grid shelf on the floor of the ROASTING OVEN and slide in the muffin tin. Slide the COLD PLAIN SHELF on to the third set of runners and bake for 20–25 minutes or until the muffins are golden. Remove from the tin and cool on a wire rack.

Conventional Baking:

Pre-heat the oven to 200ºC/400ºF/gas 6 and bake for 20–25 minutes as above.

banana and chocolate chip muffins

makes 12

360 g plain flour	200 g chocolate chips
240 g unrefined golden caster sugar	3 large eggs, slightly beaten
2 tsp baking powder	118 ml vegetable oil
1 tsp baking soda	3 large bananas, peeled and mashed
pinch of salt	

1 Line a muffin tin with muffin papers and set aside.

2 Mix together all the dry ingredients in a large bowl and all the wet in another bowl.

3 Make a well in the dry ingredients, add the bananas and pour in the wet ingredients. Using a large rubber spatula, fold the mix together using as few strokes as possible. Spoon the mix into the papers, filling them half-full if using a topping (see page 33) or to the top if not.

4 Put the grid shelf on the floor of the ROASTING OVEN and slide in the muffin tin. Slide the COLD PLAIN SHELF on to the third set of runners. Bake for 20–25 minutes or until golden. Remove from the tin and cool on a wire rack.

Conventional Baking:

Pre-heat the oven to 200ºC/400ºF/gas 6 and bake for 20–25 minutes as above.

pumpkin apple streusel muffins

This streusel topping can also be used on most other muffins.

makes 12–18

300 g plain flour
400 g unrefined golden caster sugar
1 tsp ground cinnamon
½ tsp ground ginger
½ tsp ground cloves
1 tsp baking powder
pinch of salt
2 eggs, lightly beaten
110 ml sunflower oil

235 g pumpkin purée (you can use tinned pumpkin purée)
100 ml milk
2 apples, peeled, cored and finely chopped

FOR THE STREUSEL TOPPING:
2 tbsp plain flour
60 g unrefined golden caster sugar
½ tsp ground cinnamon
20 g unsalted butter

1 Line a muffin tin with muffin papers and set aside.

2 In a large mixing bowl, combine the dry ingredients, and then add the wet and finally the apples. Stir well so that everything is thoroughly combined. Spoon the mix into the muffin papers until they are about half-full.

3 Mix the topping ingredients together and sprinkle over each muffin.

4 Bake on the fourth set of runners in the ROASTING OVEN for 20 minutes. Slide the COLD PLAIN SHELF on to the second set of runners after about 10 minutes or sooner if the muffins are browning too quickly. For 4-oven Aga owners, bake the muffins on the third set of runners in the BAKING OVEN for 20 minutes. The muffins are done when a skewer comes out clean.

Conventional Baking:

Pre-heat the oven to 180ºC/350ºF/gas 4 and bake for 35–40 minutes.

pumpkin muffins

makes 12

425 g can puréed pumpkin
3 large eggs, slightly beaten
350 g plain flour
118 ml vegetable oil
270 g unrefined golden caster sugar

2 tsp baking powder
1 tsp baking soda
pinch of salt
1 tsp pumpkin pie spice (see page 15)

1 Line a muffin tin with muffin papers and set aside.

2 Mix together all the ingredients thoroughly. Spoon the mix into the muffin tin, filling the papers to the top.

3 Put the grid shelf on the floor of the ROASTING OVEN and slide in the muffin tin. Slide the COLD PLAIN SHELF on to the third set of runners and bake for 20–25 minutes or until golden. To test if they are cooked in the middle, insert the point of a knife or a skewer and if it comes out clean they are ready. If the mix is still loose, put them back in for a few more minutes.

Conventional Baking:

Pre-heat the oven to 190ºC/375ºF/gas 5 and bake for 20–25 minutes.

cranberry, orange and pecan muffins

makes 12

220 g plain flour	zest of 1 organic orange
180 g unrefined golden caster sugar	1 large egg, slightly beaten
1 tsp baking powder	118 ml vegetable oil or melted butter
pinch of salt	160 ml milk
½ tsp cinnamon	75 g fresh cranberries
75 g chopped pecans	

1 Line a muffin tin with muffin papers and set aside.

2 Mix together all of the dry ingredients in a large bowl and all the wet in another bowl.

3 Make a well in the dry ingredients, add the cranberries and pour in the wet ingredients. Using a large rubber spatula, fold the mix together using as few strokes as possible. Spoon the mix into the muffin papers, filling them half-full if using a topping (see page 33) or to the top if not.

4 Put the grid shelf on to the floor of the ROASTING OVEN and put in the muffin tin. Slide the COLD PLAIN SHELF on to the third set of runners and bake for 20–25 minutes or until they are golden. Remove from the tin and cool on a wire rack.

Conventional Baking:

Pre-heat the oven to 200°C/400°F/gas 6 and bake for 20–25 minutes as above.

orange muffins

makes 6

145 g plain flour	2 large eggs, slightlybeaten
75 g whole wheat flour	60 ml sunflower oil
130 g unrefined golden caster sugar	2 tsp vanilla extract
2 tsp baking powder	zest of 1 large organic orange
110 ml soured cream	

1 Line a muffin tin with muffin papers and set aside.

2 Mix together all the dry ingredients in a large bowl and all the wet in another bowl. Make a well in the dry ingredients, add the zest and pour in the wet ingredients. Using a large rubber spatula, fold the mix together using as few strokes as possible.

3 Spoon the mix into the muffin papers, filling them half-full if using a topping (see page 33) or to the top if not.

4 Put the grid shelf on to the floor of the ROASTING OVEN and put in the muffin tin. Slide the COLD PLAIN SHELF on to the third set of runners and bake for 20–25 minutes or until they are golden. To test if they are cooked in the middle, insert the point of a knife or a skewer and if it comes out clean they are ready. If the mix is still loose put them back in for a few minutes more. Remove from the tin and cool on a wire rack.

Conventional Baking:

Pre-heat the oven to 190°C/375°F/gas 5 and bake for 20 minutes.

right: cranberry, orange and pecan muffins

savoury baking

savoury shortcrust pastry

makes enough for a 20.5 cm tart tin

180 g plain flour (or 100 g plain flour and 80 g rice flour, or indeed all rice flour for a very short crumbly pastry)

salt, if using unsalted butter

60 g cold butter, cubed

1 egg, beaten

1 Sift the flour and salt, if using, into the food processor, then add the butter and process for 30 seconds.

2 Add the egg and process again until it forms a ball. Stop immediately, wrap in cling film and rest in the fridge for a minimum of 30 minutes.

3 After the pastry has rested, roll it out. Line a tart tin, then let it rest again in the fridge for 30 minutes. Fill and bake according to the recipe. You could prepare a couple of pastry-lined tins and pop them into the freezer to save time.

quick polenta and pancetta pan bread

serves 4–6

75 g unsalted butter

130 g cubed pancetta

30 g honey

220 ml milk

2 eggs

180 g plain flour

100 g polenta

1 tbsp baking powder

½ tsp sea salt

1 Place the butter into a heatproof bowl and melt at the back of the Aga while you gather the rest of the ingredients.

2 Place the pancetta cubes in a cast iron frying pan and fry them on the floor of the ROASTING OVEN until they start to brown. Set aside.

3 Make the polenta bread. Beat all the wet ingredients together in a bowl. Mix the dry ingredients together in another bowl, then, whisking, pour the wet into the dry and stir well with a wooden spoon to combine. Take care not to over-mix.

4 Pour the bread batter over the pancetta. Slide the grid shelf on to the floor of the ROASTING OVEN. Place the frying pan on the grid shelf and bake for 20 minutes or until the bread is golden. Remove from the oven, invert the bread on to a plate and cut into pie slices. This is delicious with soup.

Conventional Baking:

Fry the pancetta on the hob. Pre-heat the oven to 220°C/425°F/gas 7 and bake for 20–25 minutes or until golden.

walnut and raisin bread

makes 2 loaves – eat one, freeze one!

40 g fresh yeast
700 ml hand-hot water
1 kg strong white flour
250 g rye flour

30 g salt
100 g walnuts, roughly chopped
100 g plump raisins

1 Mix the yeast into the water.

2 Fit the dough hook on to an electric mixer (you can do this by hand but it will be hard work) and put the flours and salt into the bowl of the mixer. Turn the mixer to a medium speed, then pour in the yeast and water. When the dough starts to come together, add the walnuts and raisins. Knead for about 10 minutes on a medium speed. The dough has been kneaded enough when it is smooth and pliable.

3 Place the dough into a lightly oiled large bowl, cover with a clean damp tea towel and put next to the Aga. Leave it to prove for 45–60 minutes or until it has doubled in size.

4 Knock back the dough by punching the air out and shape into loaf tins or into a round ball or long loaf on a piece of Bake-O-Glide on a baking sheet. Leave it to prove again for 30–45 minutes.

5 Slide the tins or Bake-O-Glide directly on to the floor of the ROASTING OVEN and bake for 20–25 minutes. It is ready when you tap the underside and it sounds hollow. Cool on a wire rack.

Conventional Baking:
Pre-heat the oven to 220ºC/425ºF/gas 7 and bake in the centre of the oven for 30–40 minutes or until the bread sounds hollow when tapped on the underside.

baked camembert with walnut bread

serves 6

2 x 220 g wooden boxes of ripe, ready-to-eat
Camembert
3 ripe pears, cut into quarters

12 organic dates, stones removed
1 loaf of walnut and raisin bread (see above),
sliced thinly

1 Remove the wrapping from the cheeses and place the cheeses back into the boxes. Discard the box lids.

2 Place the boxes on a baking tray and slide on to the third set of runners in the ROASTING OVEN for 10–15 minutes or until very soft.

3 While the cheese is in the oven, arrange the fruit and walnut bread on two platters, leaving space in the centre for the cheese boxes. Place a baked cheese on each platter and serve immediately. Scoop out the cheese with a spoon.

Conventional Baking:
Pre-heat the oven to 200ºC/400ºF/gas 6 and bake for 10–15 minutes or until very soft.

onion and parma ham bread

makes 1 large loaf

1 large onion, peeled and chopped into small pieces	FOR THE TOPPING:
30 g yeast	1 tbsp fresh rosemary, chopped
550 ml warm water, plus more if needed	1 tbsp thyme leaves
1 kg strong flour	1 tbsp fennel top, chopped
30 g sea salt	2 garlic cloves, sliced
118 ml olive oil	sea salt
175 g Parma ham, torn into strips	olive oil

1 Spread out the onion on a shallow baking tray lined with Bake-O-Glide. Put the tray on the third set of runners in the ROASTING OVEN and cook for 8–10 minutes until the onion is soft and slightly charred around the edges. Set aside.

2 Crumble the yeast into the warm water and mix until smooth. Put the flour and salt into the bowl of an electric mixer with the dough hook in place. Start the motor and slowly pour in the yeast mixture, then the olive oil. Add the onion and Parma ham and knead until it becomes smooth and elastic. Don't be alarmed if it looks sloppy to begin with as it will pull together.

3 Lightly grease a large bowl. Turn out the dough into it, cover with a damp tea towel and place the bowl next to the Aga for about an hour or until the dough has doubled in size.

4 While the dough is proving, mix together the herbs, garlic, salt and enough olive oil to slacken the mixture.

5 When the bread has had its first proving, knock it back by punching the air out. Line the large roasting tin with a large piece of Bake-O-Glide and shape the dough into the tin, stretching it to fit. Pour over the herb oil and, using your fingers, press the oil and herbs into the dough, giving it a dimpled effect. Leave the tin next to the Aga again for its second proving.

6 When the dough has doubled in size, place the tin on the floor of the ROASTING OVEN for 20–25 minutes. Place a stainless steal cup filled with cold water next to the bread to create steam in the oven. If it browns too quickly, insert the COLD PLAIN SHELF on the second set of runners. Cool the bread in the tin for a few minutes, then remove the Bake-O-Glide and move to a wire rack to finish cooling.

Conventional Baking:

Pre-heat the oven to 200ºC/400ºF/gas 6 and proceed as above. If you have a fan-assisted oven or electric oven, do not put the cup of water in the oven.

right: onion and parma ham bread

stuffed olive focaccia bread

Read the whole recipe before starting as you have to assemble or roast the vegetables, make the tomato sauce and make the dough. If you wish, you can save time by buying fresh tomato sauce from the chilled section of a good deli or supermarket and buy a jar of roasted vegetables in olive oil. The tomato sauce can also be used on pizzas or with pasta. It can be made ahead and kept in the fridge for 3 days or frozen.

serves 6 as a starter or 4 for lunch

FOR THE BREAD DOUGH:
30 g yeast
550 ml warm water, plus more if needed
1 kg strong flour
30 g sea salt
125 g good quality stoned black olives, chopped
118 ml olive oil

FOR THE FILLING:
approximately 600 g of a selection of grilled peppers, courgettes, red onions, sun-dried tomatoes in oil, or anything else that takes your fancy
3 x 150 g balls mozzarella cheese, grated or thinly sliced

FOR THE TOMATO SAUCE:
3 tbsp olive oil
1 garlic clove, peeled
50 g tin anchovies in olive oil plus the oil
500 g good quality peeled tinned plum tomatoes
1 tbsp balsamic vinegar
1 bunch basil leaves
1 tsp sugar
salt and pepper

1 Crumble the yeast into the warm water and mix until smooth. Put the flour and salt into the bowl of an electric mixer with the dough hook in place. Start the motor and slowly pour in the yeast mixture, then the olives and olive oil. Knead until it becomes smooth and elastic. Don't be alarmed if it looks sloppy to begin with as it will pull together.

2 Lightly grease a large bowl and turn the dough out into it. Cover with a damp tea towel and place the bowl next to the Aga for about an hour or until the dough has doubled in size.

3 When the bread has had its first proving, knock it back by punching the air out. Line a large inverted baking tray with two pieces of Bake-O-Glide. Divide the dough in half and shape both halves into rounds on the Bake-O-Glide, stretching it to fit if necessary. Leave the tin next to the Aga for 15 minutes to allow it to rise a little.

4 Place one round of the partially risen dough on the tin on the edge of the floor of the ROASTING OVEN and pull the Bake-O-Glide towards the back of the oven and the tray away so that you are left with one dough round

on the Bake-O-Glide on the oven floor. Bake for 8–10 minutes. Set the other dough round aside.

5 Meanwhile, make the sauce. Put the olive oil, garlic and anchovy oil in a heavy bottomed saucepan and heat gently on the SIMMERING PLATE. Watch it carefully and remove the garlic clove just as it starts to turn golden. (If it burns or goes brown the sauce will taste terrible.) Next add the anchovies, tomatoes, balsamic vinegar, half the basil and the sugar. Season with pepper (the anchovies are salty so don't add any salt at this stage). Stir well and bring up to a simmer. Move the pan on to the third set of runners in the ROASTING OVEN for 20–25 minutes or until the sauce is well cooked, very soft and reduced to a thick consistency. Add the remaining basil and check the seasoning.

6 When the bread base is cooked, remove from the oven and build up the layers of 'stuffing' on the baked dough in this order: grilled vegetables, cheese, tomato sauce.

7 Take the raw dough and put it on top of the filling. Wrap the dough over the top of the stuffing and around to the bottom of the baked crust and pinch on the

bottom so there is no visible seam. The filling should be sandwiched between the baked dough and the raw dough. Transfer the bread to the floor of the SIMMERING OVEN (still on the Bake-O-Glide) and bake for 1–1½ hours. If the top browns too quickly, slide in the COLD PLAIN SHELF.

8 Cool in the tin for a few minutes, then remove the Bake-O-Glide and move to a wire rack to finish cooling.

Cut into wedges and serve. This is ideal for picnics and lunch boxes.

Conventional Baking:
Pre-heat the oven to 220°C/425°F/gas 7 and bake the base for 8–10 minutes, then lower the temperature to 150°C/300°F/gas 2 and bake the stuffed bread for 1–1½ hours. Make the sauce on the hob.

focaccia bread

makes 1 loaf

30 g yeast	FOR THE TOPPING:
550 ml warm water, plus more if needed	1 tbsp fresh rosemary, chopped
1 kg strong flour	1 tbsp thyme leaves
30 g sea salt	1 tbsp fennel top, chopped
118 ml olive oil	2 garlic cloves, peeled and sliced
	sea salt
	olive oil

1 Crumble the yeast into the warm water and mix until smooth. Put the flour and salt into the bowl of an electric mixer with the dough hook in place. Start the motor and slowly pour in the yeast mixture, then the olive oil. Knead until it becomes smooth and elastic. Don't be alarmed if it looks sloppy as it will pull together.
2 Lightly grease a large bowl and turn out the dough into it. Cover with a damp tea towel and place next to the Aga for about an hour or until doubled in size.
3 While the dough is proving, mix together the herbs, garlic, salt and enough olive oil to slacken the mixture.
4 When the bread has had its first proving, knock it back by punching the air out. Line the large roasting tin with a large piece of Bake-O-Glide and shape the dough in the tin, stretching it to fit. Pour over the herb oil and, using your fingers, press the oil and herbs into the dough, giving it a dimpled effect. Leave the tin next to the Aga again for its second proving.
5 When the dough has doubled in size, place the tin on the floor of the ROASTING OVEN for 20–25 minutes. If it browns too quickly, insert the COLD PLAIN SHELF on to the second set of runners. Cool in the tin for a few minutes, then remove the Bake-O-Glide and move to a wire rack to finish cooling.

Conventional Baking:
Pre-heat the oven to 220ºC/425ºF/gas 7 and bake for 30–35 minutes.

baked polenta with garlic and parmesan

serves 6

200 g polenta
90 g Parmesan cheese, grated
2 garlic cloves, peeled and crushed

60 g butter, cubed
30 g raclette cheese, grated

1 Make up the polenta following the manufacturer's instructions.

2 When it has cooked for the required time, beat in 60 g of the Parmesan cheese. Spread the polenta out on to a shallow baking tray and let it cool and set.

3 Cut it into rounds with a cookie cutter and arrange slightly overlapping in a buttered ovenproof dish. Sprinkle over the garlic, the cubed butter and the remaining cheeses.

4 Bake on the third set of runners in the ROASTING OVEN for 20–25 minutes or until crisp and golden. For 4-oven Aga owners, bake on the third set of runners in the BAKING OVEN for 30 minutes.

5 Remove from the oven and cool on a wire rack.

Conventional Baking:

Pre-heat the oven to 200ºC/400ºF/gas 6 and bake for 15–20 minutes.

cheese and bacon puffs

serves 4

500 g shop-bought puff pastry
100 g pack cubed bacon
a little oil
Dijon mustard
125 g Gruyère cheese, grated

FOR THE EGG WASH:

1 egg yolk, beaten with a little double cream

1 Roll out the pastry into a very thin rectangle and cut in half. Transfer both pieces to a baking tray lined with Bake-O-Glide and chill in the fridge.

2 Fry the bacon in a little oil in a pan on the SIMMERING or BOILING PLATE until it is crispy, then drain on kitchen paper.

3 Remove the pastry from the fridge. Spread some mustard over it, leaving a border of about 1.5 cm. Sprinkle some of the cheese over half of each rectangle, then add the bacon and another layer of cheese. Brush a little oil over the edges of the pastry, fold over the pastry and seal the edges by pressing down firmly. You can refrigerate the puffs at this point if you wish.

4 When you are ready to bake the pastries, brush the tops with a little egg wash and bake on the floor of the ROASTING OVEN for 8–10 minutes or until puffed up and golden. Serve with green salad.

Conventional Baking:

Pre-heat the oven to 190ºC/375ºF/gas 5 and bake for 10–12 minutes.

roasted vegetable tarte tatin

serves 4–6

FOR THE PIE CRUST:

342 g plain flour

226 g butter, softened

salt and pepper

80 g Parmesan cheese, grated

1 large egg

FOR THE ROASTED VEGETABLES:

2–3 parsnips, peeled and cut into thick log shapes

2–3 carrots, peeled and cut like the parsnips

2 red onions, peeled and quartered

1 tbsp olive oil

1 tbsp unrefined golden caster sugar

2 tbsp fresh rosemary, chopped

salt and pepper

FOR THE GLAZE:

1 tbsp butter

1 tsp balsamic vinegar

1 tbsp pomegranate molasses (see page 47)

1 egg yolk, beaten

1 Make the pastry in a food processor or by hand. Process the flour with the butter until the mixture resembles coarse breadcrumbs. Add the salt, pepper, cheese and egg. Process until the dough just comes together. Tip it out on to a floured surface and knead lightly until smooth. Wrap in a plastic bag and rest in the fridge for 1 hour.

2 Meanwhile, place the parsnips and carrots in a saucepan of water and bring to the boil on the BOILING PLATE. Drain off all the water, then transfer to the SIMMERING OVEN and cook for about 12 minutes. They need to be just cooked and not too soft.

3 When ready, put the carrots, parsnips and onions into a bowl and pour over the olive oil. Add the sugar and rosemary, season and toss together to coat everything well. Spread the vegetables out on a shallow Aga baking tray and roast on the first set of runners in the ROASTING OVEN for 15–20 minutes. Move the tray to the floor of the ROASTING OVEN for a further 15–20 minutes or until the vegetables are charred around the

edges. Set aside to cool. (This can be done 24 hours in advance if you wish.)

4 When you are ready to assemble the tarte tatin, put the butter, balsamic vinegar and pomegranate molasses into the tarte tatin tin. Place it on the SIMMERING PLATE until it has all melted and cook for about 2 minutes. Take off the heat and assemble the vegetables around the bottom of the tin.

5 Roll out the pastry on a lightly floured surface to a thickness of 5 mm. Drape the pastry over the vegetables and tuck in excess pastry loosely around the side, leaving a little space so that air can escape. Brush the top of the pastry with a little beaten egg yolk.

6 Bake on the floor of the ROASTING OVEN for 35–40 minutes, sliding the COLD PLAIN SHELF on the third set of runners after 20 minutes.

Conventional Baking:
Pre-heat the oven to 200ºC/400ºF/gas 6 and bake the tarte for 40–45 minutes

pomegranate molasses

250 ml fresh pomegranate juice
140 ml honey
½ cinnamon stick

1 crushed star anise
½ tsp ground black pepper
2 tbsp balsamic vinegar

Bring all the ingredients to a simmer in a saucepan on the SIMMERING PLATE and reduce the liquid until it is thick and syrupy. Sieve into a jug, then pour into a bottle. Can be kept in the fridge for 1 month.

baked leek and squash frittata

You will need a deep dish – my tarte tatin dish is perfect!

serves 4–6

2 large leeks, washed and sliced
olive oil
7 eggs
425 g tin puréed pumpkin, or purée your own

60 ml crème fraîche
½ tbsp fresh rosemary, chopped
salt and pepper
60 g toasted pine nuts

1 Put the leeks on to a baking tray and drizzle with a little olive oil. Slide the tray on to the first set of runners in the ROASTING OVEN and bake for about 10 minutes or until they are soft.

2 Grease the tarte tatin dish with some more olive oil and set aside.

3 In a large jug mix together the eggs, pumpkin, crème fraîche, rosemary, salt and pepper. Fold in the leeks and pine nuts and pour into the tarte tatin dish.

4 Bake on the grid shelf on the third set of runners in the ROASTING OVEN for about 10 minutes or until set. For 4-oven Aga owners, put the grid shelf on the third set of runners in the BAKING OVEN and bake for about 15 minutes.

5 Remove from the oven and serve the frittata either straight away or at room temperature. Cut into thick wedges and serve with a green salad and a drizzle of pumpkin oil.

Conventional Baking:
Pre-heat the oven to 200ºC/400ºF/gas 6 and bake the leeks for 10 minutes. Turn the temperature down to 180ºC/350ºF/gas 4 and bake the frittata for 10–15 minutes or until set.

tomato and gruyère tart

This recipe can also be made as four individual tarts by cutting the pastry into smaller circles and placing on a shallow tray lined with Bake-O-Glide.

serves 4

butter, for greasing
500 g good quality store-bought puff pastry
1 tbsp Dijon mustard
250 g Gruyère cheese, grated

bunch of basil
3 large vine ripened tomatoes, very thinly sliced
salt and pepper

1 Lightly butter a 20.5 cm tart tin with a removable base.

2 Roll out the puff pastry and line the tart tin.

3 Spread the mustard over the base of the pastry, then sprinkle over the cheese. Scatter half of the basil leaves over the cheese, then top with the tomato slices. Season with salt and pepper.

4 Bake the tart on the floor of the ROASTING OVEN for 25–30 minutes or until puffed up and golden. Slide the COLD PLAIN SHELF in directly over the tart about 10 minutes into the baking time.

5 Remove the tart from the oven and stand on a cooling rack for 15 minutes. Remove from the tart tin and scatter over the remaining basil leaves. Serve warm or at room temperature with a watercress salad.

Conventional Baking:
Pre-heat the oven to 190°C/375°F/gas 5 and bake for 20–25 minutes.

right: tomato and gruyère tart

pizza dough

makes 2 pizzas

40 g fresh yeast
125 ml milk, at room temperature
175 ml hand-hot water
300 g '00' flour

40 g strong plain flour
3 g salt
olive oil, for greasing the bowl

1 Prove the yeast with the milk and water by crumbling yeast into liquid and leaving for 10 minutes.

2 Mix the yeast with the sifted flours and salt and knead for 10 minutes. The dough should be sticky.

3 Knead for a further 10 minutes, adding more flour if necessary. Whatever happens, do not end up with stable dough! It should be threatening to stick to the sides of the bowl.

4 Let it rise in an oiled bowl set close to the Aga for about 1 hour or until doubled in size.

5 Shape the dough into a pizza shape – pull and stretch, but do not roll.

6 Let it rise for about 10 minutes, then add your chosen toppings and bake (see below).

roasted beetroot pizza

makes 2 pizzas

1 quantity pizza dough (see above)

FOR THE TOPPING:
10 baby beetroot
olive oil
balsamic vinegar
salt and pepper

125 g ball buffalo mozzarella cheese, grated or thinly sliced
100 g Taleggio cheese, thinly sliced
½ tbsp fresh thyme
½ tbsp fresh rosemary, chopped

1 Cut the beetroot in half and put on a baking tray. Drizzle over some olive oil and balsamic vinegar, and season with salt and pepper. Slide on to the second set of runners in the ROASTING OVEN and roast for 15–20 minutes or until slightly charred and softish.

2 When you are ready to assemble the pizza, turn a large baking tray upside down and line with Bake-O-Glide. Pull half the pizza dough on the Bake-O-Glide into a circle. Scatter the base of the dough with half the mozzarella, then spread over half the roasted beetroot. Top the beetroot with half the Taleggio slices and herbs.

3 Carefully slide the Bake-O-Glide directly on to the floor of the ROASTING OVEN, pulling the upturned baking tray away as you do so. Bake the pizza for about 12 minutes or until puffed up and golden. Repeat for the second pizza. I like to make one pizza and share it while it is hot and cook the next one while we are eating.

Conventional Baking:

Pre-heat the oven to 200°C/400°F/gas 6 and roast the beetroot as above. To cook the pizza, pre-heat the oven to its highest setting. If you have a pizza stone, use it according to the manufacturer's instructions. Bake for 25–30 minutes.

pumpkin and taleggio calzone

serves 4 for lunch, 6 for a starter

FOR THE DOUGH:	FOR THE FILLING:
40 g fresh yeast	500 g pumpkin, peeled and deseeded
125 ml milk, at room temperature	olive oil
175 ml hand-hot water	salt and pepper
300 g '00' flour	100 g Parma ham, sliced very thinly
40 g strong plain flour	150 g Taleggio cheese, sliced
3 g salt	100 g mozzarella, sliced
olive oil, for greasing the bowl	50 g sun-dried tomatoes, chopped
	100 g wild rocket leaves

1 Prove the yeast with the milk and water by crumbling yeast into the liquid and leaving for 10 minutes.

2 Mix the yeast with the sifted flours and knead for 10 minutes – the dough should be sticky. Add more flour if necessary, but whatever happens do not end up with a stable dough! It should be threatening to stick to the bowl.

3 Place the dough in a bowl greased with oil and leave next to the Aga for about 1 hour or until doubled in size.

4 Meanwhile, cut the pumpkin into small chunks, place in a shallow baking tray, drizzle with olive oil and season with salt and pepper. Hang the baking tray on the second set of runners in the ROASTING OVEN and roast for 20–25 minutes or until the pumpkin is soft and charred around the edges. Remove from the oven and set aside.

5 Shape the dough into two rectangles.

6 Roughly divide the pumpkin and the rest of the ingredients in half. Spread each pizza with one of the halves of filling. Start with the pumpkin, spread the Parma ham on top, then layer the cheeses, tomatoes and rocket, leaving a 1–2 cm border.

7 Starting at one end of the rectangle, roll up the dough as you would for a roulade and roll it on to a piece of Bake-O-Glide (you may need to flour your hands). Make sure the seam side is down and the ends are tucked and pressed in.

8 Leave to prove for about 5–10 minutes, then slide the Bake-O-Glide directly on to the floor of the ROASTING OVEN. Cook the calzone for about 20–25 minutes or until golden and crisp. Check after 10 minutes and slide in the COLD PLAIN SHELF if browning too much.

9 Remove from the oven and cool for a few minutes, then slice and eat.

Conventional Baking:

Pre-heat the oven to 220ºC/425ºF/gas 7 and bake in the middle of the oven for 25–30 minutes.

salami, olive and mozzarella calzone

serves 4 for lunch

1 quantity pizza dough (see page 50)
olive oil
120 g salami, sliced
100 g pepperoni, sliced

30–40 g oil-marinated black olives, pitted
8 sun-dried tomatoes
150 g ball buffalo mozzarella cheese

1 Prepare the pizza dough to stage 5 (see page 50) and drizzle with olive oil.

2 Lay the salami and pepperoni over the dough base leaving a 4 cm gap around the edge. Scatter over the olives and sun-dried tomatoes. Tear the mozzarella into chunks and place on top. Roll the dough up, tuck in the ends and place on the baking tray with the seam underneath. Let it rise for 30 minutes near the Aga.

3 Put the baking tray directly on to the floor of the ROASTING OVEN and cook for 20–25 minutes or until puffed up and golden.

4 Remove from the oven and cool a little before slicing and serving. This is great for picnics.

Conventional Baking:

Pre-heat the oven to its highest setting. If you have a pizza stone, use it according to the manufacturer's instructions. Bake for 25–30 minutes, as above.

cheat's calzone

The quantities of salami and mozzarella for the filling can vary according to what you have in the fridge.

serves 4

1 tbsp chopped oregano
1 tbsp chopped chives
juice of ½ a lemon
3 tbsp sunflower oil
salt and pepper

1 ciabatta loaf or French stick
1 packet salami
1 ball mozzarella cheese
6–8 sun-dried tomatoes

1 To make the dressing, whisk together the oregano, chives, lemon juice, sunflower oil salt and pepper.

2 Split open the bread and remove some of the dough in the middle. Spread the dressing over the bread and then layer the salami, cheese and sun-dried tomatoes on the bottom half, repeating the layers until all the ingredients are used up.

3 Cover with the top half of the bread and then wrap the loaf very tightly in cling film. Press it down with tins or other heavy objects and refrigerate overnight.

4 When you are ready to serve, remove the cling film, re-wrap in foil and place it in the ROASTING OVEN for about 10 minutes until the cheese starts to ooze, then serve straight away.

Conventional Baking:

Pre-heat the oven to 200°C/400°F/gas 6 and bake the calzone as above.

right: salami, olive and mozzarella calzone

chicken and petit pois pie

You will need a stock pot or large saucepan that fits in the roasting oven and a large ovenproof dish to make the pie in.

serves 4–6

FOR COOKING THE CHICKEN:

1 medium-sized chicken, about 1½–2 kg

2 bay leaves

1 large onion, peeled and cut into chunks

6 peppercorns

1 small bunch fresh thyme
(reserve ½ tbsp of chopped leaves)

2 carrots, peeled and trimmed

enough chicken stock to cover the chicken

FOR THE FILLING:

2 tbsp sunflower oil and a little butter

150 g button mushrooms

1 medium onion, peeled and sliced

1 large leek, trimmed and sliced into chunks

2–3 tbsp flour

50 ml crème fraîche

200 g petit pois, frozen or fresh

zest of 1 lemon

1 tbsp freshly chopped flat leaf parsley

salt and pepper

1 quantity of savoury shortcrust pastry (see page 38)

FOR THE EGG WASH:

1 egg yolk mixed with a little double cream

1 Place the chicken, bay leaves, onion chunks, peppercorns, the thyme on the stalks and carrots into a large stock pot and cover with the chicken stock, adding water if the stock is very concentrated. Bring to the boil on the BOILING PLACE for 5 minutes, then transfer to the ROASTING OVEN for about 1 hour or until the juices run clear and the chicken is cooked.

2 When the chicken is cooked, remove it from the liquor and reserve the stock. Skin the chicken, take it off the bone and shred it into strips. Set aside. Strain the stock and pour into a jug. Slice the carrots and add to the chicken meat.

3 Heat the oil and butter in a large frying pan in the ROASTING OVEN and fry the mushrooms and onions until soft and just starting to colour, then add the leek and cook until soft.

4 Move the frying pan to the SIMMERING PLATE. Sprinkle the flour over the vegetables and stir with a wooden spoon until all the flour is absorbed into the fat. Slowly pour in the stock to make the gravy. You will only

need about 500 ml of stock (reserve the rest for another dish). Bring up to the simmer and cook for 3–4 minutes until it thickens.

5 Stir in the crème fraîche and petit pois. Add the chicken strips, carrots, lemon zest, chopped parsley and reserved thyme to the pan, stir well and season to taste. Transfer the pie filling to a large ovenproof dish and set aside.

6 Roll out the pastry and cover the pie dish, tucking in any overlapping pastry to form a thick rustic crust around the dish. Make a slit in the top and brush with the egg wash. Bake the pie on the fourth set of runners in the ROASTING OVEN for 30–35 minutes until golden. Slide in the COLD PLAIN SHELF if the pie browns too quickly. Serve piping hot.

Conventional Baking:

Pre-heat the oven to 200ºC/400ºF/gas 6 and cook the chicken for 1 hour or until the juices run clear. Bake the pie at the same temperature for 35–40 minutes.

focaccia cake

This recipe is really an assembly operation and could be made with good quality, store bought ingredients.

serves 6–8 as a starter or canapé

FOR THE LEMON OREGANO DRESSING:

juice of 2 lemons

5 tbsp extra virgin olive oil

salt and pepper

1 tbsp capers

2 garlic cloves

2 tbsp oregano

1 round loaf of focaccia bread, freshly baked (see page 44)

250–300 g jar roasted peppers in olive oil

8–10 slices of a mixture of Italian salami and Parma ham

250–300 g jar sun-dried tomatoes in olive oil

250–300 g jar roasted artichokes in olive oil

1 organic lemon

1 large bunch of basil leaves

FOR THE 'ICING':

500 g mascarpone cheese

1 tbsp pesto

salt and pepper

olives and cherry tomatoes for garnishing

1 To make the dressing, whizz all the ingredients together in a food processor and keep in a jar. It will last up to a week in the fridge.

2 Slice the focaccia loaf horizontally into three even layers. Brush a little of the lemon dressing on to the bottom layer and spread with the peppers, half the meats, half the sun-dried tomatoes, half the artichokes, some of the basil leaves and a drizzle more of the dressing. Cover with the middle layer of bread. Brush the middle layer with some of the dressing, repeat with the rest of the ingredients and add the final layer of bread.

3 Wrap the bread tightly in cling film. Weigh it down with a plate and set aside while you make the 'icing'.

4 Put the mascarpone, pesto and salt and pepper into a bowl and beat until smooth with an electric mixer (I use my Kitchen Aid with the paddle attachment).

5 Unwrap the cake from the cling film and transfer it to a serving plate. Using a palette knife, 'ice' the cake with the mascarpone mix, then chill in the refrigerator until it is firm. This can be assembled 1 day in advance, if you wish. Serve the cake garnished with olives and cherry tomatoes.

golden croustades

Croustades can be made in regular sized muffin tins or mini muffin tins. They are so versatile that you can fill them with almost anything – hot or cold. They can be made 1 day in advance or frozen for up to 2 weeks.

makes as many slices as in the loaf

1 loaf organic bread, thinly sliced with crusts removed

3–4 tbsp melted butter or olive oil

1 Using a rolling pin, roll out each slice of bread and brush with the butter or oil. Gently press one slice of bread into each section of a muffin tin until all the holes are lined.

2 Bake in the ROASTING OVEN for 5–8 minutes or until golden brown. Remove from the tins and cool. Fill with your choice of filling.

3 If you want to use them with a hot filling, bake until just beginning to turn brown then fill with something like a frittata mix and return to the ROASTING OVEN to bake for a further 5–8 minutes. They are also wonderful holders for baked eggs.

Conventional Baking:
Pre-heat the oven to 180°C/350°F/gas 4 and bake for 6–8 minutes or until golden.

herbed popovers

These are wonderful with crème fraîche and smoked salmon. If you make them in a mini muffin tin they can be filled and used as a base for canapés.

makes 6

vegetable oil, for coating the muffin tin
165 g plain flour
½ tsp salt
3 eggs

250 ml milk
1 tbsp vegetable oil
1 heaped tbsp chopped herbs of your choice, e.g. chives, dill, basil, etc.

1 Lightly grease a 6-hole muffin tin with some oil and place it in the ROASTING OVEN while you make up the batter.

2 Sift the flour into a large bowl, then add the remaining ingredients and mix well so there are no lumps.

3 Remove the tin from the oven and ladle in the batter. Bake on the third set of runners in the ROASTING OVEN for 15–20 minutes or until golden and puffed up.

4 Remove from the oven and immediately prick each popover with a knife to let the steam escape. Return to the oven and bake for another 5 minutes, then serve straight away.

Conventional Baking:
Pre-heat the oven to 200°C/400°F/gas 6 and bake the popovers as above.

right: golden croustades

ricotta torta

serves 8

olive oil	1 tbsp rice flour
2 large onions, peeled and finely chopped	1 kg ricotta cheese
zest and juice of 1½ lemons	4 eggs
125 g breadcrumbs	60 g Parmesan cheese, grated
1 tbsp raisins	handful of basil
1 tbsp flat leaf parsley, chopped	salt and pepper
2 tbsp pine nuts, toasted and chopped, plus 1 tbsp toasted but not chopped	

1 To make the breadcrumbs, put some olive oil into a large frying pan and heat it in the ROASTING OVEN. Move to the SIMMERING PLATE and fry a tablespoon of the chopped onion in it until soft. Add the lemon juice and zest and cook until the juice evaporates. Add the breadcrumbs and fry until golden, then add the raisins, parsley and chopped pine nuts. Transfer to a plate lined with kitchen paper and set aside.

2 In the same frying pan, pour in a little more oil and fry the rest of the onion until soft. Transfer to a bowl and cool to room temperature. (Steps 1 and 2 can be done the day before.)

3 When the onions are cool, add the rice flour, ricotta, eggs and Parmesan. Tear the basil into strips and add. Season with salt and pepper and mix well.

4 Line the base of a loose-bottomed 20.5 cm tin with Bake-O-Glide and spoon over half of the breadcrumbs. Ladle in the ricotta mixture and top with the remaining breadcrumbs.

5 Start the torta on the grid shelf on the floor of the ROASTING OVEN for 20–30 minutes with the COLD PLAIN SHELF directly above it. Remove the torta and plain shelf from the ROASTING OVEN and transfer the shelf to the third set of runners in the SIMMERING OVEN. Place the torta on the plain shelf and continue cooking for 1½–2 hours or until puffed up, checking every so often.

6 For 4-oven Aga owners, start the torta on the grid shelf on the floor of the ROASTING OVEN for 10 minutes, then move the torta to a grid shelf on the floor of the BAKING OVEN and cook for a further 1–1½ hours or until puffed up. If it browns too quickly, slide the COLD PLAIN SHELF over the torta.

7 Remove the torta from the oven and allow to cool to room temperature. Scatter with the remaining toasted pine nuts and serve with a tomato salad dressed with olive oil and balsamic vinegar.

Conventional Baking:

Cover the top of the torta with a damp piece of greaseproof paper. Pre-heat the oven to 180ºC/350ºF/gas 4 and bake for 1–1½ hours or until puffed up.

left: ricotta torta

onion seed tart filled with asparagus and lemon

serves 4–6

FOR THE PASTRY:	FOR THE FILLING:
180 g plain flour	4 large eggs
1 tsp salt	2 tbsp double cream
90 g cold unsalted butter, cubed	salt and pepper
30 g onion seeds	1 tbsp tarragon, slightly chopped
1 egg, beaten	1 tbsp lemon juice
	8–10 thin asparagus spears, bottoms peeled and trimmed
	zest of 1 organic lemon, cut into long thin strips

1 To make the pastry, sift the flour and salt into the food processor, then add the butter and half of the onion seeds and process for 30 seconds. Add the egg and process again until it forms a ball. Stop immediately, wrap in cling film and rest in the fridge for a minimum of 30 minutes.

2 Line a 23 cm square tart tin with the rest of the onion seeds so that they will provide an extra crunch and texture to the tart shell.

3 After it has rested, roll out the pastry. Line the tart tin, then rest again in the fridge for 30 minutes (you could prepare a couple of tins and pop them into the freezer).

4 To make the filling, whisk the eggs, cream, salt, pepper, tarragon and lemon juice together in a jug and pour into the pastry case. Arrange the asparagus on the filling along with the lemon zest. Place the tart on the floor of the ROASTING OVEN with the COLD PLAIN SHELF on the fourth set of runners. Bake for 20–25 minutes.

5 Remove from the oven and cool in the tin on a wire rack. Serve at room temperature.

Conventional Baking:

Pre-heat the oven to 190°C/375°F/gas 5 and blind-bake the tart shell for 15 minutes. Remove and cool for about 5 minutes, then pour in the filling and proceed as above. Lower the oven to 180°C/350°F/gas 4 and bake for 20 minutes.

right: onion seed tart filled with asparagus and lemon

onion tart

serves 4–6

75 g butter	1 quantity of savoury shortcrust pastry (see page 38)
2 tbsp olive oil	4 eggs
4 large onions, peeled and very thinly sliced	560 ml double cream
3 sprigs fresh thyme, wrapped in one layer of muslin	salt

1 Melt the butter and oil in a large, deep frying pan. Add the onions and thyme. Gently cook the onions until they are soft and brown. You can either do this on the SIMMERING PLATE or in the ROASTING OVEN – it can be useful to do this on the Simmering Plate if this is the only thing you will be cooking as it will lower the temperature in the oven for cooking the tart later on.

2 Drain the onions and remove the thyme. Set the onions aside.

3 Line a 20.5 cm tart tin with the pastry and put it in the fridge to rest for 30 minutes.

4 When you are ready to assemble the tart and bake it, beat the eggs and cream together. Season with salt, add the drained onions to the egg mix and stir well. Spoon the onion filling into the pastry case.

5 Place the tart on the floor of the ROASTING OVEN and bake for 20 minutes, sliding in the COLD PLAIN SHELF halfway through the baking time. (You can also bake this tart very slowly in the SIMMERING OVEN. When I do it this way, I usually blind-bake the case for 10 minutes in the ROASTING OVEN, add the filling, continue baking on the floor of the ROASTING OVEN for 10 minutes, then move to the SIMMERING OVEN for about an hour or even longer.) The tart should still be wobbly when you remove it from the oven. If it is runny, bake for 5 more minutes but the main thing is not to over-cook it.

6 Cool on a wire rack. Try not to refrigerate the tart – serve it on the same day.

Conventional Baking:
Pre-heat the oven to 200ºC/400ºF/gas 6. Prick the base of the pastry in the tin and blind-bake the pastry case for 10–15 minutes. It should be only lightly coloured. Turn down the oven to 140ºC/275ºF/gas 1 and bake the filled pastry case for 1–1½ hours.

parmesan tuiles

makes about 6 tuiles

175 g Parmesan cheese, grated	1 tbsp flour

1 Mix the Parmesan and the flour in a bowl.

2 Place a piece of Bake-O-Glide on the SIMMERING PLATE. Drop a spoonful of the mixture on to the Bake-O-Glide and cook for about 1 minute, then turn over and cook the other side for 1 minute.

3 Cool the tuile on a piece of kitchen paper, roll up and eat immediately! Repeat with the remaining mixture.

Conventional Cooking:
Use a non-stick frying pan over a medium hob heat.

roasted tomato tarts

serves 6

1.5 kg organic tomatoes	1 garlic clove, peeled
60 ml olive oil	500 g good quality puff pastry
40 ml balsamic vinegar	1 egg yolk, beaten
1 level tbsp sugar	18 pitted Kalamata olives
salt and pepper	

1 Cut the tomatoes into small pieces and place in a single layer on a large baking tray.

2 Pour the olive oil, balsamic vinegar, sugar, salt and pepper into a bowl and whisk well. Pour this over the tomatoes and put the garlic clove on to the tray. Place the baking tray on the second set of runners in the ROASTING OVEN and roast for 20 minutes, then move to the SIMMERING OVEN and continue to roast for a further 40–60 minutes or until they are browned and the juices are syrupy. Discard the garlic clove.

3 Roll out the puff pastry to a thickness of approximately 5 mm. Cut it into 6 rounds, each about 12 cm in diameter. Fold over 2 cm of the pastry to form a border around the edge, pressing down firmly. Transfer the tart rounds to a large baking tray lined with Bake-O-Glide.

Brush the pastry edges with beaten egg yolk.

4 Spoon the roasted tomatoes into the pastry and top each tart with 3 olives. Slide the baking tray on to the floor of the ROASTING OVEN and bake for about 10 minutes. Slide in the COLD PLAIN SHELF and continue baking for a further 8–10 minutes until the tarts are puffed up and golden.

5 Cool the tarts on a wire rack and serve at room temperature with a rocket and Parmesan salad.

Conventional Baking:
Pre-heat the oven to 190°C/375°F/gas 5. Roast the tomatoes for 1 hour or until browned and with syrupy juices. Turn the temperature up to 200°C/400°F/gas 6 and bake the tarts for 15–18 minutes.

pumpkin tarte tatin

serves 6 for a starter or 4 for lunch

FOR THE PASTRY:	FOR THE FILLING:
75 g plain flour	40 g unsalted butter
50 g chickpea flour	1 tsp brown sugar
50 g unsalted butter, at room temperature and chopped into pieces	3 whole sprigs fresh rosemary, about 10 cm long
25 g Parmesan cheese, grated	½ tsp dried chilli flakes
1 tsp fresh rosemary, chopped	1 kg pumpkin, peeled and deseeded, cut into 1 cm-thick half-moon slices
black pepper	1 tbsp balsamic vinegar, plus extra for drizzling
1 large egg	salt and pepper

1 First make the pastry. I usually use a food processor but you can do it by hand. Put the flours and butter into the food processor and pulse until it resembles coarse breadcrumbs. Add the cheese, chopped rosemary and pepper and pulse for a couple of seconds until the mix resembles fine breadcrumbs. Add the egg and pulse again for a few seconds or until soft dough is formed. Flatten the dough into a disc shape, wrap in cling film and refrigerate for at least 30 minutes.

2 Put the butter and sugar into a 27 cm tarte tatin dish. Place the dish on the floor of the ROASTING OVEN and heat until the butter sizzles.

3 Transfer the dish to the SIMMERING PLATE, place the rosemary sprigs on the bottom and scatter over half of the chilli flakes. Arrange the pumpkin slices carefully over the base of the dish, overlapping and filling in the gaps – what you see now will eventually be the top of the tart so make it look as good as possible. Season the pumpkin with salt, pepper and the remaining chilli flakes and spoon over the balsamic vinegar.

4 Transfer the dish back to the ROASTING OVEN floor and cook for 10 minutes, then cover the dish with foil and slide in a grid shelf on the fourth set of runners. Move the dish to the grid shelf and bake for another 20–25 minutes or until the pumpkin is soft, then remove the foil and place the dish on the SIMMERING or BOILING PLATE for a few minutes to reduce and thicken the juices.

5 Meanwhile, remove the pastry from the fridge and roll out into a circle large enough to cover the tarte tatin dish – about 27 cm round.

6 Take the dish off the heat and carefully lay the rolled out pastry over the pumpkin slices, tucking the pastry around the inside of the dish. (It is important to tuck the pastry in loosely to allow little gaps for the steam to escape, otherwise you'll end up with soggy pastry.)

7 Return the dish to the third set of runners in the ROASTING OVEN and bake for 20–25 minutes. If the pastry browns too quickly, slide in the COLD PLAIN SHELF just above. When the pastry is golden, remove the tarte tatin from the oven and allow to cool in the dish for about 10 minutes.

8 Place a flat plate over the dish and, protecting your hands, invert the plate and give it a gentle shake. Remove the tatin dish. If some of the pumpkin gets stuck, just ease it off the bottom and slot it into place. Shave over some more Parmesan, drizzle with good balsamic vinegar and serve with a green salad.

Conventional Baking:

Melt the butter on the hob over a medium–high heat. Add the pumpkin to the pan and cook for 10 minutes. Continue as above and cook the tart in an oven pre-heated to 200°C/400°F/gas 6 for 40–45 minutes or until the pastry is golden and cooked.

right: pumpkin tarte tatin

cakes, tarts and teabreads

banana teabread

serves 6

2 tbsp milk	1 tsp baking powder
2 eggs, beaten	150 g unrefined golden caster sugar
80 ml sunflower oil	80 g chopped walnuts or 100 g chocolate chips
3 bananas, peeled and mashed	or 60 g desiccated coconut
250 g self-raising flour	

1 Line a 900 g loaf tin with Bake-O-Glide.

2 Whisk the milk, eggs, oil and mashed bananas together in a bowl, then add the dry ingredients and mix well. Spoon the batter into the loaf tin.

3 Slide the grid shelf on the floor of the ROASTING OVEN and the COLD PLAIN SHELF above. Place the tin on the grid shelf and bake for 25–30 minutes. Transfer the now hot plain shelf to the SIMMERING OVEN, place the loaf tin on top of it and bake for a further 20 minutes or until the tea bread is done. For 4-oven Aga owners, bake in the BAKING OVEN for 50–60 minutes using the COLD PLAIN SHELF if it browns too quickly.

Conventional Baking:

Pre-heat the oven to 190°C/375°F/gas 5 and bake for 50–60 minutes.

courgette teabread

serves 6

435 g self-raising flour	200 ml sunflower oil
1 tsp salt	300 g unrefined golden caster sugar
1 tsp baking powder	300 g grated courgettes
generous grating of nutmeg	3 eggs
3 tsp cinnamon	3 tsp vanilla extract
150 g chopped walnuts	

1 Line a 900 g loaf tin with Bake-O-Glide.

2 Mix all the ingredients together in a large bowl and spoon into the loaf tin.

3 Bake the teabread on the fourth set of runners in the ROASTING OVEN for 10 minutes, then transfer to the SIMMERING OVEN for 1–1½ hours or until done. You can also cook this teabread in the Cake Baker in the ROASTING OVEN for 1 hour, or in the BAKING OVEN for 1 hour using the COLD PLAIN SHELF above if necessary.

Conventional Baking:

Pre-heat the oven to 180°C/350°F/gas 5 and bake for 1–1½ hours.

right: banana teabread

sweet pastry

TO LINE ONE 20.5 CM TART TIN:

75 g icing sugar

2 egg yolks

120 g unsalted butter, at room temperature

½ tsp baking powder

pinch of salt

250 g plain flour

2 tbsp cold water

TO LINE TWO 20.5 CM TART TINS:

172 g icing sugar

4 egg yolks

256 g unsalted butter, at room temperature

1 tsp baking powder

pinch of salt

520 g plain flour

4 tbsp cold water

1 Mix together the sugar, egg yolks, butter, baking powder and salt in a large bowl. Sift the flour on to the buttery mix and rub it together until it is sandy in texture.

2 Add the water and quickly press it into a soft dough. I usually tip it on to a clean surface to mix together. Wrap the dough in cling film and refrigerate overnight or freeze.

apple pie

serves 8

FOR THE PASTRY:

720 g plain flour

240 g unrefined golden caster sugar

pinch of salt

360 g cold unsalted butter, cubed

3 eggs, beaten (you may need 4 if the pastry is too dry)

FOR THE FILLING:

65 g flour

½ tsp ground cinnamon

½ tsp ground cardamom

half a nutmeg, grated

60 g unsalted butter, cold and cubed

60 g unrefined golden caster sugar

1 kg cooking apples, cored, peeled and chopped

1 egg yolk, beaten

1 Sift the flour, sugar and salt into the food processor, then add the butter and process for 30 seconds. Add the eggs and process again until it forms a ball (you may have to add a little cool water 1 tablespoon at a time if the mixture is dry). Stop the food processor, wrap the pastry in cling film and rest in the fridge for a minimum of 30 minutes.

2 Line a 27 cm pie dish with the pastry and chill in the refrigerator for 30 minutes. Roll out the leftover pastry to make a lid.

3 Put the flour, spices, butter and sugar into the food processor and pulse until crumbly. Transfer to a bowl and add the apples. Tip the apple mix into the lined pie dish and roll the pastry lid on top, pinching the edges of the pie together with your fingers.

4 Brush with the egg yolk and bake the pie on the floor of the ROASTING OVEN with the COLD PLAIN SHELF on the fourth set of runners for 35–40 minutes or until the crust is golden.

Conventional Baking:

Pre-heat the oven to 200ºC/400ºF/gas 6. Blind-bake the pastry-lined pie dish for 10–15 minutes, then fill and bake as above.

lemon meringue pie

For a deeper filling and meringue topping, simply double the ingredients.

serves 6

1 small quantity sweet pastry (see page 70)

FOR THE MERINGUE:
3 egg whites
176 g unrefined golden caster sugar

FOR THE FILLING:
45 g cornflour
75 g unrefined golden caster sugar
237 ml water
zest and juice of 3 large organic lemons
3 large egg yolks

1 Roll out the pastry. Line a 20.5 cm pie tin with it and prick the bottom with a fork. Place the pie tin on the floor of the ROASTING OVEN and slide the COLD PLAIN SHELF on to the third set of runners. Bake the pie crust for 8–10 minutes or until it is cooked and golden. Remove from the oven and cool a little.

2 Slide the PLAIN SHELF into the SIMMERING OVEN on the fourth set of runners.

3 Make the filling. Mix the cornflour and sugar together in a small bowl. Add 2 tbsp of the water and mix to a smooth paste.

3 Bring the remaining water to the boil in a saucepan on to the BOILING PLATE. Transfer the saucepan to the SIMMERING PLATE and, whisking all the time, pour in the cornflour paste and then add the lemon zest and juice. Whisk until the mix starts to thicken – it needs to

have the consistency of thick custard. Remove it from the heat and, still whisking, add the egg yolks one at a time. Pour the filling into the piecrust and set aside.

4 Make the meringue. Whisk the egg whites in a clean bowl with an electric whisk, adding the sugar 1 tbsp at a time, until they are at the stiff peak stage. Spread the meringue over the filling.

5 Place the pie on the PLAIN SHELF in the SIMMERING OVEN and bake for 40–45 minutes, until the meringue is set and slightly coloured. Cool the pie and serve.

Conventional Baking:

Pre-heat the oven to 190°C/375°F/gas 5 and blind bake the pastry case for 20 minutes or until cooked. Lower the temperature to 150°C/300°F/gas 2 and bake the filled pastry case for 40–45 minutes.

open apple and pear pies

serves 4

FOR THE PASTRY:	FOR THE FILLING:
360 g plain flour	65 g flour
120 g unrefined golden caster sugar	½ tsp ground cinnamon
pinch of salt	60 g cold unsalted butter, cubed
180 g cold unsalted butter, cubed	60 g unrefined golden caster sugar
2 eggs, beaten	750 g cooking apples, cored, peeled and chopped
	750 g pears, cored, peeled and chopped
	150 g quince cheese, chopped into tiny pieces
	1 egg yolk, beaten

1 To make the pastry, sift the flour, sugar and salt into the food processor, then add the butter and process for 30 seconds. Add the eggs and process again until it forms a ball (you may have to add a little cool water 1 tablespoon at a time if the mixture is dry). Stop the food processor immediately, wrap the pastry in cling film and rest in the fridge for a minimum of 30 minutes.
2 Put the flour, cinnamon, butter and sugar into the food processor and pulse until crumbly. Transfer to a bowl, add the fruit and quince cheese and toss together.
3 Roll out the dough into 4 medium-sized rounds and transfer to a baking sheet lined with Bake-O-Glide. Pile some of the filling on to each pastry round, leaving a 5 cm border. Carefully fold the border over the fruit, pleating it to make a circle. Brush with the egg yolk.
4 Bake the open pies on the floor of the ROASTING OVEN with the COLD PLAIN SHELF on the fourth set of runners for 20–25 minutes or until the crust is golden.

Conventional Baking:
Pre-heat the oven to 200ºC/400ºF/gas 6 and bake as above.

right: open apple and pear pies

pumpkin pie

serves 6–8

1 small quantity sweet pastry (see page 70)

3 eggs, beaten

425 g pumpkin purée

175 g light brown sugar

½ tsp salt

½ tsp cinnamon

½ tsp ground ginger

½ tsp ground cloves

good grating of nutmeg (about ½ tsp)

275 ml evaporated milk

1 Line a 27 cm tart tin with the pastry.

2 Whisk all the remaining ingredients together and pour into the prepared tart tin.

3 Place the pie on the floor of the ROASTING OVEN and slide the COLD PLAIN SHELF on to the third set of runners. Bake for 35–40 minutes, turning the pie around after 20 minutes. The pie is cooked when a skewer inserted in the middle comes out clean.

4 Cool on a wire rack and serve with whipped cream.

Conventional Baking:

Pre-heat the oven to 220°C/425°F/gas 7. Blind-bake the pastry case for 10–15 minutes before filling and baking for a further 40–45 minutes.

coconut cream pie

serves 6

1 small quantity sweet pastry (see page 70)

FOR THE FILLING:

3 eggs

135 g unrefined golden caster sugar

60 ml double cream

200 g desiccated coconut

1 Line a 27 cm pie dish with pastry and chill in the fridge.

2 To make the filling, beat the eggs with the sugar and add the cream, then the coconut. Spoon it into the lined pie dish.

3 Place the pie on the floor of the ROASTING OVEN and slide in the COLD PLAIN SHELF on to the fourth set of runners and bake the pie for 25–30 minutes. Cool on a wire rack. This is good served with a warm chocolate sauce.

Conventional Baking:

Pre-heat the oven to 190°C/375°F/gas 5 and blind-bake the pastry for 10–15 minutes. Fill the tart and continue to bake for 30–40 minutes.

rhubarb tart

serves 6

1 small quantity sweet pastry (see page 70)
500 ml water
30 g unrefined golden caster sugar
1 vanilla pod, split and seeds scraped out
4–6 sticks of rhubarb, cut into 4 cm chunks

60 g unsalted butter, softened
60 g icing sugar
60 g ground almonds
1 egg
15 ml double cream

1 Line a deep 20.5 cm tart tin with the pastry and chill in the fridge.

2 Put the water, caster sugar and the vanilla seeds scraped from the pod into a saucepan and bring to the boil on the SIMMERING PLATE. Add the rhubarb pieces and poach for about 1–2 minutes, or until tender but not too soft. When cooked, remove from the pan with a slotted spoon and set aside. Do not discard the poaching liquor.

3 Combine the butter, icing sugar, almonds, egg and cream in a bowl and whisk with an electric hand whisk to form a thick paste. Pour the mixture into the pastry case and top with the rhubarb.

4 Place the tart on the floor of the ROASTING OVEN and cook for 20 minutes until puffed up and golden.

Check after 10 minutes and use the COLD PLAIN SHELF on the last set of runners if the tart is browning too quickly.

5 While the tart is baking, bring the poaching liquor to the boil and simmer until it has reduced by half. Pour the juices into a jug and reserve.

6 Remove the tart from the oven and cool on a wire rack. Serve at room temperature with crème fraîche and the reduced poaching juices.

Conventional Baking:

Pre-heat the oven to 190ºC/250ºF/gas 4 and blind-bake the pastry cake for 10–15 minutes, then add the filling and bake for 30 minutes. Reduce the juices on the hob.

plum crumble tart

serves 6–8

1 small quantity sweet pastry (see page 70)

4–6 plums, stoned and cut into wedges

FOR THE CRUMBLE TOPPING:

55 g plain flour

30 g malt flour

160 g vanilla sugar (see page 15)

100 g unsalted butter, cut into pieces

½ tsp ground cloves or cinnamon

85 g chopped hazelnuts

FOR THE HAZELNUT FILLING:

58 g unsalted butter, softened

58 g icing sugar

58 g ground hazelnuts

1 egg

1 tbsp double cream

1 Line a 20.5 cm tart tin with the pastry and chill in the fridge.

2 To make the crumble topping, put the flours, sugar and butter into a large bowl and rub together so that they resemble coarse breadcrumbs. Mix in the spice and nuts.

3 To make the hazelnut filling, beat all the ingredients together in a bowl until thick. Spread over the bottom of the pastry and top with the plums. Scatter the crumble topping over the plums.

4 Place the tart on the floor of the ROASTING OVEN for 30–35 minutes. Check the tart after 20 minutes; you may need to slide in the COLD PLAIN SHELF if the top is browning too quickly. The tart should be golden brown and the pastry cooked (there is nothing more off-putting than underdone pastry!). Serve warm with clotted cream or ice cream.

Conventional Baking:

Pre-heat the oven to 190ºC/375ºF/gas 5. Blind-bake the pastry for 10 minutes. Add the filling and bake in the middle of the oven for 40 minutes or until done.

right: plum crumble tart

blueberry and frangipane tart

This can also be cooked in individual tart tins, but the total cooking time may be only 15 minutes.

serves 6

1 small quantity sweet pastry (see page 70)
58 g unsalted butter, softened
58 g icing sugar, plus extra for dusting
58 g ground almonds

1 egg
1 tbsp double cream
470 g blueberries

1 Line a 20.5 cm tart tin with the pastry.

2 Combine the butter, sugar, almonds, egg and cream to form a thick paste. Pour the mixture into the pastry case and top with the blueberries.

3 Place on the floor of the ROASTING OVEN and cook for 20 minutes until puffed up and golden. Check after 10 minutes, and slide the COLD PLAIN SHELF on to the last set of runners if the tart is browning too quickly.

4 Allow the tart to cook on a wire rack, then sift over icing sugar and serve with vanilla ice cream

Conventional Baking:

Pre-heat the oven to 190°C/375°F/gas 5 and blind-bake the pastry for 15 minutes. Cool the pastry for 10 minutes, then add the filling. Lower the temperature to 180°C/350°F/gas 4 and bake the tart for 20 minutes.

apple compôte puff pastry tarts

serves 4

50 g raisins
2 tbsp Calvados
2 large apples, peeled, cored and cut into chunks
zest of 1 lemon
pinch of cinnamon
grating of nutmeg
soft brown sugar, to taste

500 g good-quality frozen puff pastry (use French pastry if possible)
50 g pecan nuts, chopped

FOR THE TOFFEE SAUCE:
45 g unsalted butter
110 g soft brown sugar
4 tbsp double cream

1 First make the apple compôte. Soak the raisins in the Calvados for 20 minutes.

2 Put the apples into a saucepan with 1 tbsp water and the lemon zest. Cook on the SIMMERING PLATE until the apples are tender but still holding some shape.

3 Drain the raisins (keep any liquid in the bowl) and add to the apples with the spices and sugar. Leave to cool.

4 Roll out the pastry, cut into four 12 cm squares and place on a baking tray lined with Bake-O-Glide.

5 Spoon some of the compôte into each square, leaving a 2.5 cm border. Sprinkle over a little sugar and the nuts.

6 Bake on the floor of the ROASTING OVEN for 8–10 minutes or until they have puffed up and are golden.

7 Make the sauce. Put the butter, sugar, cream and any Calvados left from the raisins into a pan. Heat gently on the SIMMERING PLATE until the sugar has dissolved.

Conventional Baking:

Pre-heat oven to 190°C/375°F/gas 5 and bake as above. Make the sauce on the hob.

right: individual blueberry and frangipane tarts

treacle tart

serves 10–12

FOR THE PASTRY:	FOR THE FILLING:
300 g plain flour	540 g golden syrup
125 g cold unsalted butter, chopped	zest and juice of ½ lemon
pinch of salt	pinch of ground ginger
1 large egg	125 g soft white breadcrumbs
	70 g ground almonds
	4 egg yolks
	225 ml double cream

1 To make the pastry, put the flour, butter and salt into a food processor and process until the mix resembles fine breadcrumbs. Add the egg and 1–2 tbsp ice-cold water. Using the pulse button, process until the mixture just comes together. Flatten to a round, wrap in cling film and refrigerate for a minimum of 1 hour.

2 Roll out the pastry and line a 24 cm round tart tin. Set aside while you make the filling.

3 To make the filling, stir the golden syrup, lemon zest and juice together in a saucepan on the SIMMERING PLATE for 1–2 minutes. Whisk in the remaining ingredients and mix well. Pour into the pastry case.

4 Place the tart tin on the floor of the ROASTING OVEN, sliding the COLD PLAIN SHELF on to the third set of runners, and bake for 20–30 minutes or until the tart is slightly puffed up and starting to firm up.

5 Cool in the tin for 20 minutes, then serve with double cream or crème fraîche. This tart will keep for up to 5 days in an airtight container.

Conventional Baking:

Pre-heat the oven to 190ºC/375ºF/gas 5 and blind-bake the pastry case for 10 minutes. Fill and bake in the middle of the oven for about 40 minutes , as above.

classic chocolate cake

serves 8

150 g dark chocolate	50 g cocoa powder
125 g unsalted butter	pinch of salt
250 ml golden syrup	1½ tsp baking powder
250 ml boiling water	125 g brown sugar
350 g self-raising flour	1 large egg

1 Line a 20.5 cm square cake tin with Bake-O-Glide.

2 Melt the chocolate, butter, syrup and water in a jug.

3 Combine the flour, cocoa powder, salt, baking powder and sugar in an electric mixer, add the egg and, using the paddle attachment, start mixing. Slowly pour in the liquids and mix until the cake batter is smooth.

4 Pour the cake mix into the tin and bake on the fourth set of runners in the ROASTING OVEN for 30 minutes with the COLD PLAIN SHELF above. Transfer the now hot plain shelf and set the cake tin on it in the SIMMERING OVEN for approximately 20 minutes or until a skewer comes out clean.

5 Remove the cake from the oven and cool on a wire rack for 5 minutes. Run a knife around the edge of the tin, remove the cake and cool on a wire rack.

Conventional Baking:

Pre-heat the oven to 180ºC/350ºF/gas 4 and bake for 30–35 minutes or until the cake springs back when pressed in the centre and comes away from the sides.

chocolate chip tea cake

serves 6

90 g butter	1 egg, lightly beaten
110 g unrefined golden caster sugar	220 g self-raising flour
1 tsp vanilla extract	½ tsp baking powder
220 ml cold sour cream	100 g dark chocolate chips

1 Line a 450 g loaf tin with Bake-O-Glide and set aside.

2 Start to melt the butter in a saucepan on the SIMMERING PLATE. When it is half melted, remove from the heat and stir until fully melted. Stir in the sugar, vanilla extract, sour cream and egg.

3 Sieve the flour and baking powder together, then add to the wet mix and stir until just blended. Fold in the chocolate chips, then pour the batter into the lined loaf tin.

4 You can either use the Cake Baker to bake the cake in the ROASTING OVEN, or you can bake the loaf tin on a grid shelf on the floor of the ROASTING OVEN for 15–20 minutes, then slide in the COLD PLAIN SHELF and continue to bake for another 15–20 minutes or until it springs back when lightly pressed in the centre and is pulling away from the side. For 4-oven Aga owners, bake on the grid shelf on the floor of the BAKING OVEN for 45–50 minutes, sliding in the COLD PLAIN SHELF halfway through baking.

Conventional Baking:

Pre-heat the oven to 190ºC/375ºF/gas 5 and bake for 45–50 minutes as above.

chocolate espresso fudge cake

makes about 12 squares

85 g dark chocolate	FOR THE CHOCOLATE FUDGE ICING:
60 ml espresso	125 ml evaporated milk
240 g plain flour	150 g dark chocolate, in pieces
1 tsp baking soda	45 g unsalted butter, cut into pieces
½ tsp salt	140 g muscovado sugar
280 g muscovado sugar	1 shot (32 ml) espresso
250 ml sour cream	
85 g unsalted butter, softened	
2 eggs	

1 Line a 34.5 x 24 cm tin with Bake-O-Glide and set aside.

2 Put the chocolate and espresso into a bowl and melt at the back of the Aga while you assemble the ingredients.

3 Sift the flour, baking soda and salt into a bowl, add the sugar, then add the sour cream and butter and beat with an electric mixer for about 2 minutes.

4 Add the eggs to the batter one at a time, then add the chocolate mix and beat again until just combined.

5 Pour the mix into the tin and slide the tin on to the fourth set of runners in the ROASTING OVEN with the COLD PLAIN SHELF on the second set of runners and bake for about 20–25 minutes. You may need to turn the cake around halfway through baking. For 4-oven Aga owners, bake the cake in the BAKING OVEN on the third set of runners for about 25 minutes. To test for doneness, the top of the cake should spring back when lightly pressed.

6 Cool the cake in the tin on a cooling rack for 10 minutes, then remove from the tin and finish cooling on the rack. Ice the cake with Chocolate Fudge Icing.

7 To make the icing, bring the evaporated milk up to a boil on the SIMMERING PLATE. Remove from the heat, add the chocolate pieces and let them melt into the milk. Tip the mixture into a food processor and add the butter, sugar and espresso and process until smooth. Set the icing aside to thicken until it is the desired consistency for spreading. This is a runny icing.

Conventional Baking:
Pre-heat the oven to 180ºC/350ºF/gas 4 and bake the cake as above for 20–25 minutes. Make the icing on the hob.

chocolate hazelnut cake

serves 8

8 eggs	100 g unsalted butter, melted and at room temperature
225 g unrefined golden caster sugar	1 tsp baking powder
230 g dark chocolate, finely grated	zest of 1 organic orange
200 g ground hazelnuts	cocoa powder, for dusting

1 Line a 20.5 cm cake tin with Bake-O-Glide and set aside.

2 Whisk the eggs and the sugar on a high speed for 8–10 minutes until they look very light and fluffy and leave a thick ribbon trail.

3 Put the grated chocolate and hazelnuts into a bowl and add the melted butter, baking powder and orange zest. Combine thoroughly. Gently fold the whisked eggs and sugar into the chocolate mix so they are just incorporated. Carefully spoon the mixture into the prepared tin.

4 To bake, I strongly recommend that 2-oven Aga owners use a Cake Baker (see page 11). Bake the cake in the Cake Baker in the ROASTING OVEN for 40–45 minutes or until it is pulling away form the sides and the top springs back when lightly pressed. If you don't have a Cake Baker, start the cake off on the fourth set of runners in the ROASTING OVEN for the first 20–25 minutes, then transfer to the SIMMERING OVEN for 40–60 minutes or until done. For 4-oven Aga owners, bake in the BAKING OVEN for 40–45 minutes, sliding in the COLD PLAIN SHELF if required (check the cake after 25 minutes or so of baking).

5 When the cake is done, stand the cake tin on a wire cooling rack and cool in the tin for 15–20 minutes. Turn the cake out and finish cooling on the wire rack. Dust the cake with cocoa powder and serve.

Conventional Baking:

Pre-heat the oven to 180°C/350°F/gas 4 and bake for 40–45 minutes. Cover the top of the cake after the first 20 minutes with damp parchment paper (scrunch up the parchment paper and run it under a tap, squeeze it out and place on the cake).

flourless chocolate cake

This is a dessert cake rather than an afternoon tea cake. It will collapse and behave very badly, but it is very delicious and worth the effort. It's very rich so cut into small pieces. Serve with vanilla ice cream and chocolate sauce if you dare! This cake can be made ahead of time, turned out when cool and refrigerated.

serves 8–10

350 g good quality dark chocolate, broken into small pieces
175 g unsalted butter
6 large organic eggs
235 g unrefined golden caster sugar

FOR THE CHOCOLATE SAUCE:
100 g good quality dark plain chocolate
6 tbsp double cream
1 tsp grated orange zest

1 Line or grease the half-size roasting tin.

2 Melt the chocolate and butter together in a saucepan over a bowl of simmering water on top of the Aga.

3 Using an electric mixer, whisk the eggs and the sugar for 7–8 minutes or until very pale and fluffy. Fold the melted chocolate into the whisked eggs very gently and then pour into the prepared cake tin.

4 Bake on the fourth set of runners in the ROASTING OVEN with the COLD PLAIN SHELF on the second set of runners for 20 minutes, turning halfway through. Then transfer to the SIMMERING OVEN for another 20 minutes or until a skewer still has a bit of the cake mix stuck to it when inserted. For 4-oven Aga owners, start the cake in the BAKING OVEN with the COLD PLAIN SHELF under the cake, then transfer to the SIMMERING OVEN as above.

5 Remove from the oven and allow the cake to cool completely in the tin.

6 To make the sauce, melt the chocolate and cream over a bowl of hot water on the SIMMERING PLATE. Stir until smooth; do not allow to simmer or boil. Stir in the zest and cool until at room temperature. Serve with the cake.

Conventional Baking:
Pre-heat the oven to 180°C/350°F/gas 4. Bake the cake in a bain marie for 45 minutes. Turn off the oven and leave the oven door ajar and leave the cake sitting in the bain marie for another 30 minutes.

wheat-free chocolate sponge

The quality of the eggs used will affect the cake's flavour and texture. I use two-day-old organic free-range eggs which are perfect.

serves 4–6

150 g rice flour
25 g potato flour
1 tbsp baking powder
175 g unsalted butter, softened, or baking margarine
175 g unrefined golden caster sugar
1 shot (32 ml) of espresso or 1 tsp espresso instant coffee dissolved in 1 tbsp boiling water

3 tbsp organic cocoa powder, mixed with the espresso
3 large organic eggs

FOR THE FILLING:
whipped cream or chocolate buttercream icing (see page 104)
cocoa powder, for dusting

1 Line two 20 cm sponge tins, preferably loose bottomed, with Bake-O-Glide.

2 Put all the cake ingredients into the bowl of an electric mixer and, using the beater attachment, beat until well combined. Divide the mix between the prepared cake tins.

3 Place the grid shelf on the floor of the ROASTING OVEN and place the cake tins to the right on the grid shelf. Slide the COLD PLAIN SHELF on to the third set of runners above and bake the cakes for 20 minutes or until they are golden on top, are gently coming away from the sides and spring back when lightly pressed on top. For 4-oven Aga owners, place the cake tins on the fourth set of runners in the BAKING OVEN and only insert the cold plain shelf if the cakes are browning too quickly.

4 Remove the cakes from the oven and stand on a wire rack for a minute, then remove them from the tins and cool on the rack.

5 When the cakes are cool, spread one cake with whipped cream or chocolate buttercream icing and top with the other cake. Dust with cocoa powder and serve.

Conventional Baking:
Pre-heat the oven to 160ºC/325ºF/gas 3 and bake for 20–25 minutes.

chocolate roulade

serves 6

6 eggs, separated
100 g unrefined golden caster sugar
35 g self-raising flour

35 g cocoa powder
300 ml whipping cream

1 Line a shallow baking tray with Bake-O-Glide.

2 Whisk the egg yolks with 40 g of the sugar for about 5 minutes until they are pale. Set aside.

3 Whisk the egg whites together in a separate bowl until they reach the soft peak stage, then add the remaining sugar one tablespoon at a time until the stiff peak stage is reached.

4 Gently fold the egg yolks into the egg whites and then fold the sifted flour and cocoa into the egg mix. Spread the cake mix on to the shallow baking tray.

5 Bake on the third set of runners in the ROASTING OVEN for 8–10 minutes or until the cake springs back when gently pressed in the centre.

6 While the cake is baking, lay a clean tea towel over a wire rack and then lay a piece of greaseproof paper on top of the tea towel.

7 When the cake is done, remove it from the oven, immediately invert it on to the greaseproof and peel off the Bake-O-Glide. Allow the cake to cool completely.

8 When the cake is ready, whip the cream to soft peaks and spread over the cake. With the short end of the cake facing you, roll it carefully into a roulade. Wrap the tea towel around and secure the top with clothes pegs or a bulldog clip to hold its shape. Place in the fridge.

9 When you are ready to serve, dust with icing sugar or spread with whipped cream.

Conventional Baking:

Pre-heat the oven to 200°C/400°F/gas 6 and proceed as above.

right: chocolate roulade

gooey chocolate cake

serves 4–6

250 g good quality dark chocolate, broken into little pieces

5 eggs, separated

175 g soft brown sugar

1 tbsp Dutch processed cocoa powder

25 g plain flour

1 shot (32 ml) espresso

FOR THE ICING:

150 g cream cheese

60 g unsalted butter, softened

350 g icing sugar

1 tsp vanilla extract

2 tbsp cocoa powder

1 Line two 20.5 cm loose bottomed cake tins with Bake-O-Glide.

2 Melt the chocolate in a bowl at the back of the Aga or over a pan of simmering water.

3 While it is melting, cream together the egg yolks and the sugar in an electric mixer until they are thick and smooth. Stir the melted chocolate into the creamed egg yolks and sugar, then sift in the cocoa and flour and add the espresso. Mix well.

4 Whisk the egg whites in a clean bowl until they are at the soft peak stage, then fold 1 tbsp of the whites into the chocolate mix. Fold in well, then add the rest of the whites and fold in very carefully.

5 Pour the cake batter into the prepared tins and bake on the grid shelf on the floor of the ROASTING OVEN with the COLD PLAIN SHELF just above for 20 minutes. The cakes are done when they spring back when lightly pressed in the centre.

6 Remove from the oven and let the cakes cool completely in the tins on a wire rack.

7 For the icing, beat the ingredients together in an electric mixer, then ice the cakes and sandwich together.

Conventional Baking:

Pre-heat the oven to 180°C/350°F/gas 4 and bake as above in the middle of the oven.

slow oven chocolate cake

serves 6

225 g dark chocolate
225 g unsalted butter, softened
225 g unrefined golden caster sugar
7 eggs, separated

45 g plain flour
½ tsp baking powder
60 g ground almonds
cocoa or icing sugar for dusting

1 Line a 20.5 cm square cake tin with Bake-O-Glide.

2 Melt the chocolate in a pan at the back of the Aga.

3 Cream the butter and sugar together until light and fluffy. Whisk the egg whites in a clean bowl so they form stiff peaks. Sift the flour into a bowl and stir in the baking powder and almonds.

4 Add the melted chocolate to the egg yolks, then add them little by little to the butter and sugar mix, alternating with the flour and almond mix until it is all used up. Stir 1 tbsp of the egg whites into the mix, then carefully fold in the rest of the egg whites. Make sure there aren't any white pockets. Pour the cake mix into the prepared tin.

5 Bake on the third set of runners in the ROASTING OVEN for 10 minutes, then move to the SIMMERING OVEN for 45–60 minutes or until the cake springs back when lightly pressed in the middle and the sides are just pulling away.

6 Cool on a wire rack, then dust the cake with cocoa or icing sugar. Store in an airtight tin. The cake will last for 3 days.

Conventional Baking:

Pre-heat the oven to 190ºC/350ºF/gas 4 and bake for 10 minutes, then lower the temperature to 150ºC/300ºF/gas 2 and continue baking for 1½–2 hours.

russian shortcake

makes 12–14 pieces

145 g butter	120 g sultanas
145 g soft brown sugar	
1 tbsp golden syrup	FOR THE ICING:
1 egg	4 tbsp icing sugar
1½ tsp vanilla extract	2 tbsp butter
260 g plain flour	2 tsp golden sugar
1 tsp baking powder	1 tsp ground ginger

1 Line a deep Swiss roll tin with Bake-O-Glide.

2 Melt the butter, sugar and golden syrup together in a saucepan on the SIMMERING PLATE and cool a little.

3 Beat the egg and vanilla together in a large bowl. Stir the butter mix into the egg, add the flour, baking powder and sultanas and mix well. Pour the mixture into the tin.

4 Slide the tin on to the fourth set of runners in the ROASTING OVEN and bake for 3–5 minutes, then slide in the COLD PLAIN SHELF directly above and continue baking for a further 10 minutes. Do not over-bake. For 4-oven Aga owners, bake in the BAKING OVEN without the cold plain shelf for 10 minutes.

5 Meanwhile, make the icing. Melt all the icing ingredients in a saucepan on the SIMMERING PLATE. Ice the cake immediately it comes out of the oven and let the cake cool completely in the tin before removing.

Conventional Baking:

Pre-heat the oven to 190°C/375°F/gas 5 and bake for 15–20 minutes. Do not over-bake.

coffee and almond sponge meringue

serves 4–6

220 g unrefined golden caster sugar	1 shot (32 ml) espresso coffee or 1 tbsp instant coffee dissolved in 1 tbsp boiling water
100 g butter	1 tsp cornflour
4 large eggs, separated	50 g sliced almonds
150 g ground almonds	

1 Line a 27 cm round tin with Bake-O-Glide.

2 Combine 110 g of the sugar with the butter using an electric mixer.

3 Beat the yolks and slowly pour into the mixer, taking care not to curdle the mix. Add the ground almonds and espresso and mix well. Spread this mix into the tin.

4 Place the tin on a grid shelf on the floor of the ROASTING OVEN and bake for about 10 minutes.

5 Using a very clean bowl and an electric whisk, whisk the egg whites with the cornflour until they are at the soft peak stage, then whisk in the remainder of the sugar 1 tbsp at a time.

6 Remove the cake from the oven and carefully spread the meringue over the cake batter and sprinkle with the sliced almonds. Return the cake to the ROASTING OVEN and bake for 20–30 minutes. You will probably need to slide the COLD PLAIN SHELF on to the runners above if the meringue browns too quickly.

7 Remove from the tin and cool on a wire rack. Serve in slices with whipped cream.

Conventional Baking:

Pre-heat the oven to 200°C/400°F/gas 6 and bake as above.

date and walnut cake

serves 8–10

350 g unrefined golden caster sugar	8 egg whites
2 tsp baking powder	600 ml double cream
12 digestive biscuits, crushed into large crumbs	vanilla extract
250 g walnut halves	halved dates and walnuts, to decorate
250 g stoned dates, chopped	

1 Grease a 28 cm springform cake tin, line the base with greaseproof paper and grease again.

2 Mix all the dry ingredients together in a bowl, making sure the dates are evenly distributed though the mixture. Whisk the egg whites until they are very stiff and fold them carefully into the dry mix.

3 Pour the mix into the prepared tin. For 2-oven Aga owners, put the cake into the largest cake tin in the Cake Baker and bake for 40 minutes (check the cake after 30 minutes). For 4-oven Aga owners, bake for 40 minutes in the BAKING OVEN.

4 When the cake is cooked, remove the bottom of the tin and cool on a wire rack. Remove the paper. If the cake doesn't seem cooked, don't worry – it can sometimes appear a bit sticky. When the cake is cold, place it on a serving plate.

5 To serve, the cake cut it into slices. Whip the cream with a little of the vanilla extract to form soft peaks. Spread it over the cake slices and top with the walnuts and dates. The cake can be made 2 days in advance, but do not top with the cream, fruit or nuts until you are ready to serve.

Conventional Baking:
Pre-heat the oven to 180ºC/350ºF/gas 4 and bake for 40–45 minutes.

bottled damson cake

serves 8–10

600 g jar bottled damsons	2 tsp baking powder
250 ml sunflower oil	1 tsp almond extract
100 ml milk	
425 g unrefined golden caster sugar	FOR THE TOPPING:
3 large eggs	100 g golden syrup
550 g self-raising flour	50 g unsalted butter
100 g ground hazelnuts	80 g rolled oats
50 g semolina	80 g chopped hazelnuts
pinch of salt	

1 Drain the damsons from the bottle juices and set aside. Reserve the bottle juices for another recipe.

2 Tip the remaining cake ingredients into a large mixing bowl and mix together really well.

3 To make the topping, melt the syrup and butter in a small saucepan and then add the oats and hazelnuts.

4 Line the half-size roasting tin with Bake-O-Glide and pour in the cake mix. Spread the damsons over the cake mix, then scatter over the oat topping.

5 Slide the grid shelf on to the fourth set of runners in the ROASTING OVEN. Place the cake on the shelf, then slide the COLD PLAIN SHELF on to the second set of runners and bake for 30–35 minutes. Transfer the now hot plain shelf to the SIMMERING OVEN, place the cake on top of it and bake for another 1–2 hours or until a skewer comes out clean. For 4-oven Aga owners, use the BAKING OVEN for about 1 hour or until a skewer comes out clean.

6 Take the cake out of the oven and cool. Serve with thick double cream.

Conventional Baking:
Pre-heat the oven to 190ºC/375ºF/gas 5. Bake for 1 hour or until a skewer comes out clean.

right: bottled damson cake

gingerbread cake

serves 6–8

FOR THE TOPPING:	1 tsp ground ginger
120 g butter	½ tsp ground cloves
175 g brown sugar	½ tsp ground cardamom
3 pears, peeled, cored and sliced into quarters	pinch of salt
	1½ tsp baking soda
FOR THE CAKE	125 g unsalted butter
250 ml treacle	125 g brown sugar
250 ml boiling water	1 large egg
350 g self-raising flour	
1 tsp cinnamon	

1 Make the topping first. Melt the butter in a 27 cm tarte tatin dish on the BOILING or SIMMERING PLATE, then sprinkle over the sugar and cook undisturbed for about 3 minutes.

2 Arrange the pear quarters on the melted butter and sugar and continue cooking on the SIMMERING PLATE for about 2 minutes, then set aside.

3 To make the cake, measure the treacle into a heatproof bowl and pour the boiling water over. Mix the flour, spices, salt and baking soda together in a large bowl. In the bowl of an electric mixer cream together the butter, sugar and egg until light and fluffy. Then slowly add the dry mix 3 tbsp at a time, alternating with the treacle until it is all smooth and combined.

4 Pour the cake mix over the pears and bake on the fourth set of runners in the ROASTING OVEN with the COLD PLAIN SHELF above for 30 minutes. Transfer the cake to the SIMMERING OVEN for a further 20 minutes or until a skewer come out clean.

5 Remove the cake from the oven and cool on a wire rack for 5 minutes. Run a knife around the edge of the tin. Protecting your hands and holding a large plate over the cake, invert the cake on to the plate so that the top becomes the bottom and the pears are on top. Serve with vanilla ice cream.

Conventional Baking:

Pre-heat the oven to 180ºC/350ºF/gas 4 and bake for 40–50 minutes or until the cake springs back to the touch and is coming away from the edges.

treacle tea cake

serves 6–8

200 g unsalted butter, very soft
75 g unrefined golden caster sugar
125 g treacle
250 g self-raising flour
½ tsp bicarbonate of soda

1 tsp cinnamon
½ tsp ground ginger
4 eggs, beaten
4 pieces of stem ginger in syrup, drained of the syrup and chopped into small pieces

1 Line a 20.5 cm cake tin with Bake-O-Glide.

2 Cream the butter and sugar together, then slowly add the treacle, beating all the time (I use an electric mixer for this).

3 Sieve the flour, bicarbonate of soda and the spices together. Pour a little of the egg into the butter mix, alternating with the flour mix and ending with the flour. Fold in the ginger pieces, then spoon the mix into the prepared cake tin.

4 Slide the tin on to the third set of runners in the ROASTING OVEN with the COLD PLAIN SHELF just above and bake for 20 minutes. Then transfer the now hot PLAIN SHELF to the third set of runners in the SIMMERING OVEN and place the cake on top. Continue baking for another 40–60 minutes or until the cake is just pulling away from the sides and springs back when touched in the centre.

5 Let the cake cool in the tin for a few minutes, then turn out on to a wire rack. Dust with icing sugar and serve.

Conventional Baking:
Pre-heat the oven to 180°C/350°F/gas 4 and bake for 35–40 minutes. If the cake browns too quickly, cover the top with a piece of foil.

classic scones

makes 6–8

225 g self-raising flour
1½ tbsp unrefined golden caster sugar
pinch of salt

40 g butter, softened
150 ml milk
1 egg yolk, beaten, to glaze

1 Line a baking tray with Bake-O-Glide.

2 Combine the flour, sugar and salt in the bowl of an electric mixer with the paddle hook attached. Add the butter in pieces, then add the milk. Mix until the dough just starts to hold together. Turn out on to a floured surface.

3 Roll out the dough to a thickness of 2 cm and cut out with a fluted cutter. Put the scones on the baking tray and brush the tops with egg yolk. Sprinkle over a little more caster sugar if you wish.

4 Slide the baking tray on to the third set of runners in the ROASTING OVEN and bake for 8–10 minutes or until they are golden. Remove from the oven and cool on a wire rack.

Conventional Baking:
Pre-heat the oven to 200°C/400°F/gas 6 and bake as above.

honey and lemon madeleines

makes 12–14

250 g unrefined golden caster sugar
250 g plain flour
1 tsp baking powder
4 eggs

2 tbsp honey
zest of 1 organic lemon
250 g unsalted butter, melted

1 Grease a madeleine tin with butter and dust with flour (you can also use a mini muffin tin).
2 Put the sugar, flour, baking powder, eggs, honey and lemon zest into a bowl and whisk. Slowly pour in the melted butter, whisking all the time (I use my electric mixer for this stage).
3 Spoon about one tablespoon of the mix into each mould – the exact quantity depends on how big the depressions in the mould are.

4 Put the madeleine tin on the grid shelf on the floor of the ROASTING OVEN with the COLD PLAIN SHELF on the second set of runners and bake the cakes for 8–10 minutes or until risen and golden.
5 Remove from the tin and cool on a wire rack.

Conventional Baking:

Pre-heat the oven to 200ºC/400ºF/gas 6 and bake as above.

peach cake

You will have to use tinned peaches in winter, but in the summer choose fresh ones. In the summer I also like to mix blueberries with the peaches.

serves 6–8

425 g self-raising flour
1 tsp baking powder
240 g butter, softened
200 g unrefined golden caster sugar

3 eggs
1 tsp vanilla extract
350 g chopped peaches

1 Line a 34.5 x 24 cm tin with Bake-O-Glide.
2 Put the flour, baking powder, butter, sugar, eggs and vanilla extract into an electric mixer fitted with the paddle attachment and mix to a smooth dough. Take out one third of the dough and press the rest into the prepared tin. The dough will be sticky so you may want to press it in with your hand inside a freezer bag or wet your fingers with cold water. Spread the fruit on top and scatter with clumps of the reserved dough.

3 Slide the tin on to the fourth set of runners in the ROASTING OVEN and bake for 20–30 minutes or until done. For 4-oven Aga owners, bake in the BAKING OVEN on the third set of runners for about 30 minutes. Cool the cake in the tin.

Conventional Baking:

Pre-heat the oven to 190ºC/375ºF/gas 5 and bake for 30 minutes.

plum cake

serves 8–10

260 ml sunflower oil	1 tsp baking soda
30 ml walnut oil	2 tsp baking powder
450 g unrefined golden caster sugar	generous grating of nutmeg
3 large eggs	½ tsp cinnamon
6–8 plums, stoned and chopped into small cubes	½ tsp ground cardamom
700 g plain flour	1 tsp vanilla extract
pinch of salt	

1 Line a 20.5 cm square cake tin with Bake-O-Glide, or use the large round cake tin with the Cake Baker.

2 Tip all the ingredients into a large mixing bowl and mix together really well. Spoon into the tin.

3 Slide the COLD PLAIN SHELF on to the fourth set of runners in the ROASTING OVEN and place the cake tin on top of it. Bake for 20 minutes, then transfer the shelf to the fourth set of runners in the SIMMERING OVEN. Place the cake on the shelf and continue baking for another 30–45 minutes or until done. This cake can also be baked in the Aga Cake Baker. For 4-oven Aga owners, cook in the BAKING OVEN for about 1 hour or until a skewer comes out clean.

4 Cool in the tin, then serve with clotted cream.

Conventional Baking:

Pre-heat the oven to 190ºC/350ºF/gas 4 and bake for about 1–1½ hours.

cherry and almond cake

This is a lovely moist cake that keeps in an airtight tin for ages. It is also very good for tuck boxes and can be sent to keep hungry students going!

serves 6

230 g butter	3 eggs
230 g unrefined golden caster sugar	100 g ground almonds
230 g plain flour	120 g organic glacé cherries or griottine cherries
½ tsp baking powder	1 tsp almond extract

1 Line the base of a 20.5 cm loose-bottomed round tin with Bake-O-Glide.

2 Cream the butter and sugar together. Sieve the flour and baking powder together. Add the eggs one at a time to the creamed butter, alternating with the sieved flour to prevent the eggs from curdling. Add the ground almonds, cherries and almond extract and mix well.

3 Pour the mix into the tin. Place on the COLD PLAIN SHELF on the fourth set of runners in the ROASTING OVEN. Bake for 10 minutes, then transfer the shelf with the tin to the SIMMERING OVEN and bake for 1½–2 hours. (In some Agas this cake can take up to 5½ hours!)

Conventional Baking:

Pre-heat the oven to 130ºC/260ºF/gas ¾ and bake for 3 hours.

lemon meringue cake

serves 6

FOR THE LEMON CUSTARD FILLING:	
250 ml milk	1 tbsp lemon zest
100 g unrefined golden caster sugar	4 egg yolks
3 egg yolks	100 g plain flour
1 tbsp cornflour	1 tsp baking powder
1 tbsp plain flour	160 ml milk
60 ml lemon juice	
40 g unsalted butter, softened	FOR THE MERINGUE:
	4 egg whites
FOR THE CAKE:	½ tsp cream of tartar
110 g unsalted butter, softened	200 g unrefined golden caster sugar
110 g unrefined golden caster sugar	

1 First, make the lemon custard. Heat the milk in a saucepan on the SIMMERING PLATE until almost boiling, then remove from the heat. Whisk the sugar, yolks and flours in a bowl until the mixture is thick and pale. Gradually add the hot milk and stir until smooth.

2 Rinse out the saucepan and return the custard to it. Put it back on the SIMMERING PLATE and stir constantly until it comes to a boil and thickens. Remove from the heat and beat in the lemon juice and butter. Cover and cool to room temperature, then refrigerate until needed. This can be done in advance.

3 Line the bases of two 20.5 cm loose-bottomed cake tins with Bake-O-Glide.

4 To make the cake, cream the butter, sugar and lemon zest until light and fluffy, then add the egg yolks one at a time, alternating with the flour and baking powder. Add the milk and stir until the mix is smooth. Divide the cake batter between the prepared tins. Set aside.

5 To make the meringue, whisk the egg whites with the cream of tartar to the soft peak stage, then add the sugar little by little, whisking until it is thick, stiff and glossy. Spoon the meringue evenly over the cake batters. Place the grid shelf on the floor of the ROASTING OVEN and put the cake tins on top of it. Slide the COLD PLAIN SHELF on to the second set of runners and bake the cakes for 20–25 minutes.

6 Cool the cakes in the tins on a wire rack, then when ready to serve, place one of the cakes meringue side down and spread with the lemon custard, then place the other cake, meringue side up, on top.

Conventional Baking:

Make the custard on the hob. Pre-heat the oven to 200°C/400°F/gas 6 and bake as above.

right: lemon meringue cake

sour cream coffee cake

This cake mixture can also be used to make muffins. Fill large muffin cases with the mixture and bake as in the pumpkin muffin recipe on page 33.

serves 6–8

FOR THE STREUSEL TOPPING:
150 g chopped pecan nuts
185 g granulated sugar
1 tsp ground cinnamon

FOR THE CAKE:
240 g unsalted butter, softened, plus extra for greasing
250 g unrefined golden caster sugar

300 g self-raising flour
1 tsp baking powder
pinch of salt
2 eggs
250 ml sour cream
1 tsp vanilla extract

1 To make the topping, mix all the ingredients in a bowl and set aside.

2 Grease a 25 cm ring cake tin with butter.

3 Cream the butter and sugar together using an electric mixer. Sift the flour, baking powder and salt together in a separate bowl. In another bowl lightly beat the eggs, sour cream and vanilla extract together. Slowly add a little of the wet mix to the creamed butter, alternating with the dry until it is all used up.

4 Pour half the cake mix into the tin. Sprinkle on half the streusel mix. Add the rest of the cake mix and top with the remaining streusel.

5 Slide the COLD PLAIN SHELF on to the fourth set of runners in the ROASTING OVEN and bake for 20 minutes, then move the now hot PLAIN SHELF to the SIMMERING OVEN. Place the cake on top and continue baking for another 25–30 minutes or until done. For 4-oven Aga owners, bake in the BAKING OVEN for 35–45 minutes, sliding in the COLD PLAIN SHELF after about 20 minutes if the cake is browning too much on top.

6 Cool in the tin on a wire rack for 10 minutes, then serve the cake warm, when it will be deliciously crumbly.

Conventional Baking:

Pre-heat the oven to 180°C/350°F/gas 4 and bake as above for 45 minutes.

cider vinegar 'cheese' cake

This is called 'cheese' cake not because it is made with cheese, but because it goes so well with a thick chunk of mature Cheddar.

serves 6–8

225 g unsalted butter, cut into small pieces
450 g self-raising flour
225 g soft brown sugar
225 g sultanas

225 g dried apple pieces
3 tbsp cider vinegar
300 ml full fat milk
1 tsp bicarbonate of soda

1 Line a 23 cm round or square, deep cake tin with Bake-O-Glide.

2 Put the butter and flour into a food processor and pulse until it is the consistency of fine breadcrumbs (you can do this by hand). Transfer to a large bowl and add the sugar and dried fruit.

3 Put the milk and vinegar into a large jug, then sprinkle on the bicarbonate of soda – be careful as it will froth up so the jug needs to be deep. Add the liquid to the dry mix and stir it all together quickly.

4 Pour it into the prepared tin. For 2-oven Aga owners, either use the Cake Baker (see page 11) or start the cake off on the third set of runners in the ROASTING OVEN for 20 minutes, then transfer to the SIMMERING OVEN for 2–2½ hours. If the top browns too quickly, slide in the COLD PLAIN SHELF. For 4-oven Aga owners, start the cake off in the ROASTING OVEN for 20 minutes, then transfer to the BAKING OVEN for 1–1½ hours. Use the COLD PLAIN SHELF if it browns too quickly on top.

5 Cool in the tin. Serve with chunks of mature Cheddar cheese or slathered in butter. It will keep in an airtight tin for about 1 week. You can freeze this cake for up to 3 months, wrapped well in cling film and foil.

Conventional Baking:
Pre-heat the oven to 180ºC/350ºF/gas 4 and bake for 1–1½ hours or until done.

all-in-one wheat-free sponge

You can use either unsalted butter or good quality baking margarine in this recipe. The margarine makes the cake slightly lighter, but the butter gives it a richer taste. The quality of the eggs used will affect the cake's flavour and texture. I use 2-day-old organic free-range eggs.

serves 4–6

150 g rice flour
25 g potato flour
3 rounded tsp baking powder
175 g baking margarine or unsalted butter, softened
175 g unrefined golden caster sugar
1 tsp vanilla extract

3 large organic eggs
1 tbsp milk

FOR THE FILLING:
whipping cream and soft fruits
icing sugar, for dusting

1 Line two 20 cm sponge tins, preferably loose bottomed, with Bake-O-Glide.

2 Put all the cake ingredients into the bowl of an electric mixer and, using the beater attachment, beat until combined.

3 Divide the cake mix between the prepared cake tins. Place the grid shelf on the floor of the ROASTING OVEN and place the cake tins to the right on the grid shelf. Slide the COLD PLAIN SHELF on to the third set of runners and bake the cakes for 20 minutes or until they are golden on top, are gently coming away from the sides and spring back when lightly pressed on top. For 4-oven Aga owners, cook the cakes on the fourth set of runners in the BAKING OVEN and use the COLD PLAIN SHELF only if the cakes are browning too quickly. Remove the cakes and stand on a wire rack for a minute, then remove from the tin and cool on the rack.

4 When the cakes are cool, whip the cream to soft peaks and spread on one cake, then top with the fruits and the second cake. Dust with icing sugar and serve.

Conventional Baking:

Pre-heat the oven to 160°C/325°F/gas 3 and bake for 20–25 minutes.

all-in-one sponge cake

serves 4-6

175 g self-raising flour
175 g unsalted butter, softened
175 g unrefined golden caster sugar
1 tsp vanilla extract
3 large organic eggs
1 rounded tsp baking powder

FOR THE FILLING:
whipping cream and soft fruits
icing sugar

1 Line two 20 cm sponge tins, preferably loose bottomed, with Bake-O-Glide.

2 Put all the cake ingredients into the bowl of an electric mixer and, using the beater attachment, beat until combined. Divide the mixture between the prepared cake tins.

3 Place the grid shelf on the floor of the ROASTING OVEN and place the cake tins to the right on the grid shelf. Slide the COLD PLAIN SHELF on to the third set of runners and bake the cakes for 20 minutes or until they are golden on top, gently coming away from the sides and spring back when lightly pressed on top. For 4-oven Aga owners, cook the cakes on the fourth set of runners in the BAKING OVEN and use the COLD PLAIN SHELF only if the cakes are browning too quickly.

4 Let the cakes stand on a wire rack for 1 minute, then remove them from the tins and cool on the wire rack.

5 When the cakes are cool, whip the cream to soft peaks and spread on one cake, then top with the fruits and the second cake. Dust with icing sugar and serve.

Conventional Baking:
Pre-heat the oven to 170ºC/340ºF/gas 3½ and bake for 30–35 minutes.

icings and fillings

I am useless at icing cakes and must admit most just get a dusting of icing sugar or cocoa powder.

cream cheese icing

118 g unsalted butter, softened
300 g cream cheese
700 g icing sugar
1 tsp vanilla extract

Using an electric beater, beat the butter and cream cheese together until smooth. Slowly add the icing sugar and vanilla extract, making sure the mixture is lump-free and very smooth.

peanut butter cream icing

3 large egg whites
155 g unrefined golden caster sugar
375 g peanut butter

Place the egg whites and sugar in a large heat-proof bowl over a pan of simmering water, creating a bain marie, and whisk until the sugar has dissolved. When ready, take the bowl off the heat and, using an electric whisk, whisk the mix until it starts to form soft peaks, then add the peanut butter little by little until it is all combined. Chill until it becomes stiff but still spreadable, and then use to ice the cake.

buttercream icing

230 g icing sugar
120 g unsalted butter
1–2 tsp of a suitable extract for flavouring

Sieve the icing sugar into a large bowl and cream with the butter. Add extract for flavour. Suitable flavours include coffee powder, vanilla extract, almond extract and cocoa powder.

walnut filling

3 tbsp apricot jam   1 tsp vanilla extract

30 g walnuts, chopped   80 g ground almonds

Warm the jam at the back of the Aga and sieve it into a bowl, then mix everything together.

chocolate cake icing

75 g unsalted butter   5–6 tbsp milk

50 g cocoa powder   225 g icing sugar

Melt the butter in a saucepan at the back of the Aga. Stir in the cocoa powder and cook on the SIMMERING PLATE for a minute or so, then remove from the heat.

Stir the milk into the icing sugar, then mix well into the butter and cocoa. Cool until it has thickened, then ice your cake.

chocolate cream cheese icing

300 g cream cheese   1 tsp vanilla extract

118 g unsalted butter, softened   2 tbsp cocoa powder

700 g icing sugar

Beat everything together very well in an electric mixer, then use to ice and fill the cakes.

traybakes and
biscuits

traybakes

These are cakes made by the all-in-one method, baked and served from the tin. The method is the same whichever size you make. I use my Kitchen Aid mixer to make these cakes, but you can do it by hand if you prefer. I have developed a tin especially for traybakes (see page 11). It comes in two sizes, small (34.5 x 24 cm, depth 3 cm) and large (46 x 34.5 cm, depth 3 cm), and the quantities given here fit those tins. The small tin makes about 12 squares of cake, the large tin makes about 24. Line the tins with Bake-O-Glide.

Traybakes are the perfect recipes when you need to bake a large quantity of cakes, for example those occasions when you need to provide cakes for school events or when running a cake stall at a fair.

basic traybake mix

SMALL:	LARGE:
275 g self-raising flour	450 g self-raising flour
225 g unrefined golden caster sugar	350 g unrefined golden caster sugar
225 g unsalted butter, softened, or baking margarine	350 g unsalted butter, softened, or baking margarine
2 tsp baking powder	3 tsp baking powder
1 tsp vanilla extract	2 tsp vanilla extract
5 eggs	7 eggs

1 Put all the ingredients into the bowl of an electric mixer and mix until well combined. Pour the batter into the tin and smooth the top with a palette knife.
2 Bake the cake on the fourth set of runners in the ROASTING OVEN with the COLD PLAIN SHELF on the second set of runners. The small traybakes take 20–25 minutes to cook, the large ones 30–35 minutes. The cake is done with it springs back when lightly pressed in the middle and it pulls away from the sides of the tin.
3 Remove the cake from the oven and cool in the tin on a wire rack.

Conventional Baking:
Pre-heat the oven to 180ºC/350ºF/gas 4 and bake the small traybake for 35–40 minutes, the large one for 40–45 minutes.

Variations
The variations for this cake are endless – here are some ideas. These quantities are for the small traybakes, double up for the large.

Marmalade and ginger
Add 1 tbsp coarse cut marmalade, the zest of 1 orange, 1 tbsp honey and 1 tsp ground ginger.

Chocolate and pistachio
Add 4 tbsp cocoa powder mixed with 2–3 tbsp boiling water, 1 tbsp golden syrup, 50 g dark chocolate chips and 75 g chopped pistachio nuts.

Lemon drizzle
Add the zest of 2 lemons. Make the drizzle with the juice from the lemons and 2 tbsp of unrefined golden caster sugar brought to the boil on the SIMMERING PLATE. When the cake is warm, pour over the syrup.

Walnut and espresso with cappuccino icing

Add 2 shots of espresso (each approximately 32 ml) and 100 g chopped walnuts to the cake mixture. For the icing, beat together 75 g softened unsalted butter, 225 g icing sugar and 1 tbsp concentrated liquid coffee. Whisk 100 ml double cream to the soft peak stage, then fold in the coffee mix. Ice the cake and dust lightly with cocoa powder.

cheddar and mango chutney scone traybake

makes about 12 squares

475 g self-raising flour
1 level tbsp baking powder
pinch of salt
150 g butter, softened
2 large eggs, beaten, plus 100 ml mango chutney plus enough double cream to make 300 ml of liquid in total, including the eggs

250 g strong Cheddar cheese, grated and tossed in 1 tbsp self-raising flour

FOR THE TOPPING:
1 egg yolk, beaten with 1 tbsp milk
50 g Cheddar cheese, grated

1 Line a small traybake tray with Bake-O-Glide.
2 Combine the flour, baking powder and salt in an electric mixer with the paddle hook. Add the butter in pieces. Lightly beat the eggs, chutney, and cream together so they total 300 ml and add to the flour and butter. Add the cheese and mix until the dough just holds together.
3 Press into the traybake tin so that it is 2 cm thick and brush with the egg glaze. Mark the dough into squares. Sprinkle over the grated cheese topping.

4 Slide the tin on to the third set of runners in the ROASTING OVEN and bake for 20–25 minutes or until golden. Slide the COLD PLAIN SHELF in after 10 minutes. Remove from the oven and cool on a wire rack. Break off what you want and serve.

Conventional Baking:
Pre-heat the oven to 200°C/400°F/gas 6 and bake the scone for 20–25 minutes or until golden.

cheese and onion scone bake

makes about 10

180 g self-raising flour
1 level tbsp baking powder
pinch of salt
20 g butter, softened
1 large egg
1 tbsp double cream
2 tbsp milk

200 g strong Cheddar cheese, cut into small pieces and tossed in 1 tbsp self-raising flour
8–10 silver skin pickled onions, thinly sliced

FOR THE GLAZE:
1 egg yolk, beaten with 1 tbsp milk
30 g Cheddar cheese, grated

1 Line a baking tray with Bake-O-Glide and lightly flour.
2 Combine the flour, baking powder and salt in the bowl of an electric mixer with the paddle hook. Add the butter. Lightly beat the egg, cream and milk together. Add it to the flour and butter. Add the cheese and sliced onions and mix until the dough holds together.
3 Turn on to a baking tray, push the dough down until it is 2 cm thick and brush with the glaze. Mark the dough into squares. Sprinkle over the grated cheese topping.

4 Slide the baking tray on to the third set of runners in the ROASTING OVEN and bake for 25–30 minutes or until golden. Use the COLD PLAIN SHELF if it browns too quickly. Remove from the oven and cool on a wire rack. Break into pieces and serve.

Conventional Baking:
Pre-heat the oven to 200°C/400°F/gas 6 and bake for 15 minutes or until golden.

courgette scone bake

makes about 10

180 g self-raising flour
½ tsp baking powder
20 g butter
1 large egg, beaten
1 tbsp double cream
100 g Parmesan cheese, grated
100 g grated courgette
100 g grated carrot

salt and pepper
grating of nutmeg
100 g pancetta, cubed

FOR THE GLAZE:
1 egg yolk, beaten with 1 tbsp milk
20 g Parmesan cheese, grated

1 Line a baking tray with Bake-O-Glide and lightly flour.

2 Combine the flour, baking powder and butter in an electric mixer with the paddle hook. Lightly beat the egg and cream together. Add it to the flour and butter. Add the cheese, courgette, carrot, salt, pepper, nutmeg and pancetta and mix until the dough just holds together.

3 Turn out on to a floured surface and knead for no more than 1 minute. Roll out the dough on to the prepared baking tray to a thickness of 2 cm and brush with the egg glaze. Mark the dough into squares.

Sprinkle over the Parmesan cheese.

4 Slide the baking tray on to the third set of runners in the ROASTING OVEN and bake for 25–30 minutes or until golden. Use the COLD PLAIN SHELF if it browns too quickly. Remove from the oven and cool on a wire rack. Break off what you want and serve.

Conventional Baking:
Pre-heat the oven to 200°C/400°F/gas 6 and bake for 15 minutes or until golden.

cheese biscuits

You can freeze this dough at the 'just combined' stage. I suggest shaping it into a log and wrapping it first in greaseproof paper, then in foil to keep in the freezer. When you want to use it, simply unwrap and, using a very sharp knife, slice it into rounds and continue baking as above.

makes about 20–25 biscuits

145 g plain flour	1 tbsp thyme leaves
145 g wholewheat four	1 tbsp honey
60 g Parmesan cheese, grated	175 ml milk
2 tsp salt	1 egg white, lightly whisked
30 g unsalted butter, cut into pieces	1 tbsp nigella seeds, for sprinkling

1 Put the flours, cheese and salt into the bowl of the food processor. Pulse a couple of times to mix. Add the butter and thyme, then pulse until the mix resembles coarse breadcrumbs.

2 Mix the honey and milk in a jug, then, with the machine on slow speed, pour it through the top until the dough just comes together. Stop as soon as it does as you do not want to over-work the dough. Wrap it in cling film and refrigerate for 30 minutes.

3 Turn out the dough on to a lightly floured surface and divide into four pieces, then roll each piece very thinly. Transfer the pastry to a baking sheet lined with Bake-O-Glide and, using the cutter of your choice, cut the dough into shapes. Remove the excess dough and brush the shapes with the beaten egg white and sprinkle with some more salt and the nigella seeds.

4 Slide the baking tray on to the fourth set of runners in the ROASTING OVEN with the COLD PLAIN SHELF directly above and bake for about 10 minutes. Turn the tray and continue baking for about another 5 minutes or until the biscuits are firm to the touch and lightly coloured. For 4-oven Aga owners, slide the baking tray on to the third set of runners in the BAKING OVEN and bake for about 20 minutes, turning the tray halfway through the baking time.

5 Remove the biscuits from the oven and carefully transfer them on to a wire rack to cool.

Conventional Baking:
Pre-heat the oven to 190ºC/375ºF/gas 5 and bake in the middle of the oven for 20–25 minutes, turning the baking tray halfway through baking.

right: cheese biscuits

chocolate almond caramel bars

makes about 12 bars

150 g plain flour	FOR THE CARAMEL:
1 tsp baking powder	220 g unrefined golden caster sugar
60 g ground almonds	80 ml water
60 g unrefined golden caster sugar	80 ml double cream
125 g unsalted butter, melted	50 g unsalted butter, chopped
125 g dark chocolate, finely chopped or in chips	50 g slightly salted butter, chopped
60 ml double cream	

1 Sieve the flour and baking powder into a large bowl. Add the almonds and sugar and mix well. Pour in the melted butter and stir to combine, then press the dough into the small shallow baking tray.

2 Slide the baking tray on to the third set of runners in the ROASTING OVEN and bake for 10–12 minutes or until golden. Remove from the oven and leave to cool in the tin. For 4-oven Aga owners, bake in the BAKING OVEN on the third set of runners for 12–15 minutes.

3 Make the caramel while the base is cooling. Put the caster sugar and 80 ml water into a saucepan and stir on the SIMMERING PLATE until the sugar has dissolved. Then move to the BOILING PLATE and boil without stirring until it turns amber in colour. Remove from the heat and slowly add the 80 ml cream (watch out because it will spit) and both types of butter and stir to combine. Put it back on to the SIMMERING PLATE and simmer for 3–5 minutes. Remove from the heat and leave to stand for about 20 minutes or until it starts to thicken, then pour over the cooked pastry base. Set aside until completely cool.

4 Put the chocolate into a bowl. Pour the 60 ml of double cream into a saucepan and bring to a strong simmer on the SIMMERING PLATE, then pour over the chocolate and stir until it is well combined and all the chocolate has melted. Pour the chocolate over the cool caramel and then put the baking tray into the refrigerator for about 3 hours until set. Cut into wedges or bars.

5 Store in an airtight container in the fridge. They can be made 3 days in advance.

Conventional Baking:
Pre-heat the oven to 190°C/375°F/gas 5 and bake the dough for 12–15 minutes or until golden. Cook the topping on the hob.

pecan shortbread squares

makes about 20 bars, enough for 1 large baking tray or 2 small ones

FOR THE SHORTBREAD:

500 g butter, at room temperature

250 g unrefined golden caster sugar

515 g plain flour

125 g semolina

1 tbsp vanilla extract (optional)

FOR THE TOPPING:

500 g unsalted butter

250 ml honey

750 g brown demerara sugar

zest of 1 lemon

zest of 1 orange

60 ml double cream

1 kg pecan nuts, chopped

500 g dark organic chocolate

1 To make the shortbread, cream together the butter and sugar until pale and fluffy in an electric mixer with the paddle attachment. Sift in the flour and semolina and add the vanilla extract if using.

2 Combine well, then press the mix into one large or two small 5 cm deep baking trays, cover with cling film and refrigerate overnight.

3 Remove the cling film and bake on the fourth set of runners in the ROASTING OVEN with the COLD PLAIN SHELF on the second set of runners for 10 minutes – do not let it colour. Remove to a wire rack and allow to cool.

4 To make the topping, combine the butter, honey, sugar and zests in a saucepan and cook over a low heat until the butter has melted, stirring with a wooden spoon. Bring to a boil and boil for 2–3 minutes.

5 Remove from heat and add the cream and nuts. Stir well, then pour over the baked shortbread. Bake on the fourth set of runners in the ROASTING OVEN for 20–25 minutes with the COLD PLAIN SHELF above. For 4-oven Aga owners, bake the filled shortbread in the BAKING OVEN, as above. Cool in the tin on a wire rack.

6 Melt the chocolate in a bowl at the back of the Aga. Cut the pecan shortbread into squares, dip one half in the melted chocolate and leave to harden. Store in a cool place, wrapped in greaseproof paper.

Conventional Baking:

Pre-heat the oven to 190°C/375°F/gas 5 and bake the shortbread for 10 minutes. Turn the temperature down to 180°C/350°F/gas 4 and bake the filled shortbread for 20–25 minutes.

chocolate caramel brownies

makes about 10 brownies

300 g dark chocolate, chopped
228 g butter
342 g unrefined golden caster sugar
3 large organic eggs
2 tsp vanilla extract
110 g plain flour

2 tsp baking powder
pinch of salt (if using unsalted butter)
100 g chopped hazelnuts
350 g caramel candies, unwrapped and in pieces
2 tbsp milk

1 Melt the chocolate and butter in a bowl at the back of the Aga. Set aside to cool for about 5 minutes.
2 Stir together the sugar, eggs and vanilla extract. Pour the egg mix into the chocolate and sift over the flour, baking powder and salt. Dust the nuts with a teaspoon of flour (it stops them sinking into the mix) and add.
3 Stir the mix well, then pour into a greased baking tray to a depth of 3 cm. Bake in the ROASTING OVEN on the fourth set of runners with the COLD PLAIN SHELF above for 20 minutes. Tap the side of the tin to release any air bubbles and continue baking for a further 15 minutes.

Don't overcook as brownies should be slightly squidgy.
4 Heat the caramels with the milk in a saucepan on the SIMMERING PLATE until just melted and spreadable, then pour over the cooling brownies.
5 Cool thoroughly, then cut into squares and keep in an airtight tin or in the refrigerator. These can be made 3 days in advance.

Conventional Baking:
Pre-heat the oven to 180°C/350°F/gas 4 and bake as above.

oatmeal and coconut bars

makes 24 bars

200 g desiccated coconut
150 g plain flour
170 brown sugar
60 g granulated sugar

½ tsp salt
270 g unsalted butter, cut into pieces
75 g oatmeal
340 ml raspberry jam

1 Lightly toast 170 g of the coconut on a baking tray on the first set of runners in either the ROASTING or BAKING OVEN for 2–3 minutes, checking frequently to make sure it doesn't burn, or in a dry frying pan on the SIMMERING PLATE.
2 Using a food processor, make the dough. Blend together the flour, sugars, salt and butter. Using the pulse button, or folding in by hand, add the toasted coconut and the oatmeal.
3 Reserve 170 g of the dough and press the rest into a greased shallow baking tray. Spread the jam over, then

crumble over the remaining dough. Sprinkle over the untoasted coconut and bake on the third runners in the ROASTING OVEN for 20–25 minutes. Slide in the COLD PLAIN SHELF if the mixture browns too quickly.
4 Cool in the tray on a wire rack until it is completely cold. Lift it out and cut into bars. Can be made 3 days in advance.

Conventional Baking:
Pre-heat the oven to 190°C/375°F/gas 5 and bake for 20–25 minutes.

right: chocolate caramel brownies

lemon squares

makes 20 small squares

FOR THE BASE:	FOR THE FILLING:
250 g unsalted butter, softened	6 extra large organic eggs
125 g unrefined golden caster sugar	750 g unrefined golden caster sugar
500 g plain flour	zest of 6 lemons
pinch of salt	250 ml lemon juice
	250 g plain flour

icing sugar, for dusting

1 Line a 5 cm-deep baking tray with Bake-O-Glide.

2 To make the base, cream the butter and sugar together in a food processor until pale and fluffy. Sift in the flour and salt. Mix with paddle attachment until just combined. Make a ball out of the dough, flatten and line the baking tray. Cover with cling film and chill for a minimum of 30 minutes.

3 Bake on the fourth set of runners in the ROASTING OVEN for 10 minutes. Do not let it brown. Use the COLD PLAIN SHELF if the oven is too hot. For 4-oven Aga owners, bake in the BAKING OVEN. Allow the base to cool on a wire rack.

4 To make the filling, whisk all the ingredients together until combined, then pour on to base. Bake on the fourth set of runners in the ROASTING OVEN for 20–25 minutes or until the filling is set. Slide in the COLD PLAIN SHELF if the oven is too hot. For 4-oven Aga owners, use the BAKING OVEN.

5 Cool in the tin, then dust the top with icing sugar and cut into squares.

Conventional Baking:

Pre-heat the oven to 180°C/350°F/gas 4 and bake the base for 15–20 minutes, then cool on a wire rack. Add the filling and bake at the same temperature for 30–35 minutes.

chocolate chip biscotti

makes approximately 14

270 g self-raising flour
1 tsp baking powder
145 g unrefined golden caster sugar
200 g dark chocolate chips

pinch of salt
3 large eggs
2 tsp vanilla extract
beaten egg or milk, to glaze

1 Sieve the flour and baking powder together into a large bowl, then add the sugar, chocolate chips and salt and mix well.

2 Beat the eggs with the vanilla extract and then pour them into the dry ingredients and mix well – you can do this in an electric mixer using the paddle attachment. The dough will be very soft and slightly wet.

3 Turn out the dough and make into flattish shape on a baking sheet lined with Bake-O-Glide. Brush lightly with a little beaten egg or milk. Slide the baking tray into the ROASTING OVEN on the fourth set of runners with the COLD PLAIN SHELF above for 20–30 minutes or until golden. For 4-oven Aga owners, bake in the BAKING OVEN for 25–35 minutes.

4 Remove the loaf from the oven and cool on a wire rack. Set the lined baking tray aside.

5 When it is cool, slice the loaf diagonally into slices 2.5 cm thick. Lay the slices on the lined baking tray and bake in the SIMMERING OVEN for about 20 minutes or until the biscotti are crisp.

6 Cool on a wire rack and store in an airtight tin.

Conventional Baking:
Pre-heat the oven to 200°C/400°F/gas 6, bake the loaf for 20–30 minutes and then bake the biscotti slices for another 20 minutes.

chocolate peanut butter cookies

makes about 15 large cookies

150 g organic dark chocolate
170 g brown sugar
120 g chunky peanut butter
60 g very soft unsalted butter, at room temperature
2 large eggs

1 tsp vanilla extract
170 g plain flour
½ tsp baking powder
120 g dark chocolate chips

1 Melt the chocolate in a large bowl at the back of the Aga.

2 Combine all the ingredients together well in the bowl and drop tablespoons of the dough on to an ungreased baking sheet, spacing them well apart.

3 Bake on the fourth set of runners in the ROASTING OVEN with the COLD PLAIN SHELF on the second set of runners for 8–10 minutes or until puffed up and set to the touch. Don't over-cook. Cool on a wire rack.

Conventional Baking:
Pre-heat the oven to 190°C/375°F/gas 5 and bake for 12–14 minutes or until they are puffed up and set to the touch.

puddings and
desserts

chocolate pear crumble

serves 6

100 g butter, chilled, plus a little extra for greasing

6 ripe pears

1 tsp ground ginger

80 g plain flour

60 g ground almonds

100 g unrefined golden caster sugar

3 tbsp cocoa powder

75 g dark chocolate, chilled

1 Lightly grease a deep medium sized ovenproof dish with butter. Peel, quarter and core the pears. Cut into chunks and put into the dish. Sprinkle over the ginger.

2 In a food processor, whizz the flour, ground almonds, sugar and cocoa powder until blended. Cut the chilled butter into small pieces, add to the bowl and pulse process until it is mixed in and crumbly.

3 Coarsely grate the chilled chocolate, add to the processor and give it another quick whizz. Spread the crumble evenly over the pears.

4 Put the dish into an Aga roasting tin and hang the tin on the fourth set of runners in the ROASTING OVEN. Cook for 20–25 minutes, then transfer to the SIMMERING OVEN and cook for a further 20–25 minutes or until the fruit is tender and the topping is cooked. For 4-oven Aga owners, cook on the third set of runners in the BAKING OVEN for 35–45 minutes. Serve with vanilla ice cream.

Conventional Baking:
Pre-heat the oven to 180ºC/350ºF/gas 4 and bake for 25 minutes until golden brown.

kashmir plums

serves 6

150 ml water

45 ml organic honey

1 whole star anise

1 cinnamon stick

6 bruised cardamom pods

small pinch of saffron strands

12 ripe plums, halved and stoned

1 Place the water, honey and spices in a saucepan, bring up to the boil and simmer on the SIMMERING PLATE for 5 minutes.

2 Spread 2 large pieces of foil over a deep baking tray, forming a cross. The foil must be large enough to hold all the plums and the liquid and be gathered at the top to form a completely enclosed parcel.

3 Spread the plums on to the foil and pour over the spiced liquor. Wrap up the parcel and bake the plums on the third set of runners in the ROASTING OVEN for 25–30 minutes or until they are soft and tender.

4 Remove the plums from the oven when they are tender. Pour the liquor back into a saucepan and reduce for 3–5 minutes on the SIMMERING PLATE until it is thick and syrupy (sometimes this is not necessary as the cooking liqueur thickens within the foil). Serve 4 plum halves per person with a large dollop of crème fraîche.

Conventional Baking:
Cook step 1 on the hob. Pre-heat the oven to 200ºC/ 400ºF/gas 6 and cook as above.

sticky plum pudding

serves 6–8

200 g plums, stoned and chopped

1 tsp espresso powder or 1 shot (32 ml) espresso

1 tsp vanilla extract

1 tsp bicarbonate of soda

150 ml boiling water

85 g unsalted butter, softened, plus extra for greasing

55 ml golden syrup

85 g unrefined golden caster sugar

2 large eggs

140 g self-raising flour

30 g cocoa powder

FOR THE TOFFEE SAUCE:

60 g unsalted butter

60 g salted butter

170 g soft brown sugar

100 ml whipping cream

1 Grease a medium sized ovenproof dish with unsalted butter.

2 Put the plums, espresso, vanilla, bicarbonate of soda and boiling water into a jug and let it stand while you make the pudding.

3 Cream the butter with the golden syrup and caster sugar in an electric mixer until very pale and fluffy – it will take about 5 minutes. Turn down the speed of the mixer and beat in one egg at a time.

4 Put the flour and cocoa powder into a roomy sieve, then sieve it on to the creamed butter and sugar. Fold it in with a metal spoon, then add the plum mix to this, again folding in with the spoon. The mix will now be sloppy which is fine! Pour the pudding mix into the prepared dish.

5 Put the grid shelf on to the floor of the ROASTING OVEN and place the pudding on top. Slide the COLD PLAIN SHELF just above and bake for about 30 minutes or until it has risen and bounces back when you press the middle. For 4-oven Aga owners, place the pudding on the fourth set of runners in the BAKING OVEN and bake for 30–35 minutes, using the COLD PLAIN SHELF if it starts to brown on top.

6 Make the sauce while the pudding is baking. Chop up the two butters and put into a small saucepan with the sugar and cream. Gently heat on the SIMMERING PLATE, stirring all the time, until the sugar has dissolved and the sauce is creamy.

7 Serve the pudding hot with the sauce and lots of double cream – this pudding is not a low fat option!

Conventional Baking:

Pre-heat the oven to 190ºC/375ºF/gas 5 and bake for 20–25 minutes. Make the sauce on the hob.

poached pears with coffee

serves 6

1 litre freshly brewed medium strength coffee (or stronger if you prefer)

90 g demerara sugar

1 large cinnamon stick, broken in half

6 firm pears, peeled with stems intact

double cream, to serve

1 Put the coffee, sugar and cinnamon stick into a large saucepan. Bring up to the boil on the BOILING PLATE and stir until all the sugar dissolves.

2 Place the pears into the boiling liquid and simmer in the SIMMERING OVEN for 40–45 minutes or until they are tender.

3 Remove the pan from the heat and cool the pears in the liquid, turning them from time to time so they are evenly coloured.

4 Transfer the pears to a serving dish. Sieve the coffee liquid into a clean saucepan and bring back to the boil, then simmer to reduce until syrupy. Pour the coffee over the pears and set aside to cool.

5 When ready to serve, place pears in individual bowls, pour over the coffee syrup and serve with thick cream.

Conventional Baking:

Poach the pears on the hob over a medium heat.

chocolate brioche pudding

serves 6

255 ml milk

255 ml double cream

1 vanilla pod, split

25 g unrefined golden caster sugar

200 g dark chocolate, broken into small pieces

4 egg yolks

½ tsp cornflour

1 brioche loaf, cut into 1-cm thick slices, then into triangles

1 Put the milk, cream, vanilla pod and sugar into a saucepan on the SIMMERING PLATE and heat to just a simmer. Take off the heat and add the chocolate so that it melts, stirring occasionally.

2 In a large bowl, beat the egg yolks with the cornflour. When all the chocolate has melted, whisk the chocolate custard into the egg yolks vigorously so that the eggs do not curdle. Set aside.

3 Cover the base of a ceramic baking dish with the brioche. (You may wish to grease the dish with unsalted butter, but it is not essential.) Pour over half the custard, then add the rest of the brioche and pour over the remaining custard. Cover the dish with cling film and gently press down to soak the bread thoroughly in the custard. Set aside for 20 minutes.

4 Remove the cling film, place the dish inside a larger roasting tin and pour in hot water to come halfway up the sides of the baking dish. Slide the tin on to the fourth set of runners in the ROASTING OVEN and bake for 20–25 minutes until just set. Remove from the oven and serve warm with crème fraîche.

Conventional Baking:

Pre-heat the oven to 200ºC/400ºF/gas 6. Remove the cling film and place the baking dish into a larger roasting tin and pour in hot water to come halfway up the sides of the baking dish. Bake for about 20 minutes or until just set.

right: poached pears with coffee

bitter orange marmalade tart

serves 6

1 quantity sweet pastry (see page 70)

58 g unsalted butter, softened

58 g icing sugar

58 g ground almonds

1 egg

1 tbsp double cream

300–350 g jar bitter orange marmalade

60 g sliced almonds

1 Line a 20.5 cm tart tin with the pastry.

2 Combine the butter, sugar, ground almonds, egg and cream in a bowl to make a thick paste.

3 Spread the marmalade over the bottom of the pastry (you may not need all of it, depending on the size of the tart case). Pour the cream mixture over the marmalade case and scatter over the sliced almonds.

4 Bake the tart on the floor of the ROASTING OVEN for 20 minutes until puffed up and golden. Check after 10 minutes and slide in the COLD PLAIN SHELF on the last set of runners if the top of the tart is browning too quickly.

Conventional Baking:

Pre-heat the oven to 190ºC/375ºF/gas 5 and blind-bake the lined pastry in the tart tin for 15 minutes. Cool a little and proceed as above, baking the filled tart at the same temperature for 20 minutes.

cheesecake

serves 6

200 g digestive biscuits, smashed into crumbs

50 g chopped hazelnuts

60 g butter, melted

175 g unrefined golden caster sugar

400 g cream cheese

237 g sour cream

3 large eggs

1 vanilla pod, seeds scraped out

strawberries, for serving

1 Mix the digestive crumbs, nuts and butter in a bowl and press into a 20.5 cm springform tin. Cover with cling film and refrigerate for about 45 minutes until set.

2 Using a hand mixer, blend the sugar, cream cheese, sour cream, eggs and vanilla seeds together and pour on to the prepared biscuit base.

3 Bake the cheesecake on a grid shelf on the floor of the ROASTING OVEN with the COLD PLAIN SHELF directly above it for 20 minutes. Remove the cake and plain shelf from the Roasting Oven and transfer the plain shelf to the third set of runners in the SIMMERING OVEN. Place the cake on the plain shelf and continue cooking for 1½–2 hours, checking every so often.

4 For 4-oven Aga owners, start the cake on the grid shelf on the floor of the ROASTING OVEN for 10 minutes, then move the cheesecake to a grid shelf on the floor of the BAKING OVEN and cook for a further 1–1½ hours. If it browns too quickly, slide the COLD PLAIN SHELF over the cake.

5 Remove the cheesecake from the oven and allow to cool. Refrigerate for a few hours, then serve with a topping of fresh strawberries.

Conventional Baking:

Pre-heat the oven to 150ºC/300ºF/gas 2. Bake the cheesecake in the middle of the oven for 30 minutes, then turn off the oven and let the cake cool completely inside the oven.

banana and cardamom tarte tatin

This dish is traditionally made with apples but you can use almost any fruit. However, very soft fruit is not suitable and fruits such as plums and apricots will take longer to caramelize because of their juices. Puff pastry is usually used but the tart works just as well with home-made shortcrust. Use a tarte tatin dish. This dessert can be made up to the cooking part and kept refrigerated until you are ready to bake it, or indeed cook it early in the day and serve at room temperature.

serves 4–6

FOR THE CARAMEL:
75 g unrefined golden caster sugar
32 g unsalted butter
1 star anise

4–6 bananas, peeled and cut into 6 cm pieces (I cut mine on a slant)
135 g unrefined golden caster sugar
6 cardamom pods, cracked open
60 g unsalted butter, diced
150 g good quality bought puff pastry

1 First make the caramel. Place the sugar in the bottom of the tart tin and heat it on the SIMMERING PLATE until it turns a dark caramel colour. Take great care not to burn it. Remove it from the heat and stir in the butter and the star anise. Let it cool for a few minutes, then remove and discard the star anise.

2 Arrange the banana pieces on the caramel, packing them in very tightly. Mix the sugar with the cardamom pods and sprinkle over the bananas, then dot the butter on top.

3 Roll out the pastry large enough to cover the tatin tin. Drape the pastry over the fruit and loosely tuck it in. There needs to be room for steam to escape so that the pastry doesn't go soggy.

4 Put the tart tin on the fourth set of runners in the ROASTING OVEN and bake for 25–35 minutes or until the tart is golden and the fruit is tender. If the pastry is browning too quickly, slide the COLD PLAIN SHELF on to the second set of runners. If the juices are not sufficiently caramelized, put the tart back on the floor of the ROASTING OVEN to bake for a few more minutes.

5 When it is ready, remove the tart from the oven and let it stand for 5–10 minutes. To turn it out, place a plate on top of the tart mould and invert. Serve with thick Greek yoghurt.

Conventional Baking:
Make the caramel on the hob over a gentle heat. Pre-heat the oven to 200ºC/400ºF/gas 6 and bake the tart for 40–45 minutes.

rhubarb and orange blossom water clafoutis

serves 8

600 g rhubarb, cut into 2–3 cm pieces	1 egg yolk
250 g unrefined golden caster sugar	200 ml milk
zest of 1 lemon	200 ml double cream
1 tbsp orange blossom water	1 tsp rosewater
5 eggs, whisked	75 g plain flour

1 Place the rhubarb, 150 g of the sugar, the zest and orange blossom water in a saucepan and gently heat on the SIMMERING PLATE to dissolve the sugar. Simmer for 2–3 minutes or until the rhubarb is tender. Strain the fruit and reserve the cooking liquor.

2 Whisk the eggs, the extra yolk, the remaining sugar, the milk, cream and rosewater together until smooth, then sift in the flour and whisk again until lump-free.

3 Place the rhubarb in a large, shallow, buttered oven-proof dish or individual buttered ramekins and pour over the batter. Place the dish or ramekins on a baking tray on the third set of runners in the ROASTING OVEN for 15–20 minutes or until puffed up and golden on top.

4 Meanwhile, bring the reserved juices to the boil on the BOILING PLATE and reduce until they are syrupy. Serve the clafoutis with clotted cream and the reduced juices.

Conventional Baking:

Pre-heat the oven to 190ºC/375ºF/gas 5 and bake for 20 minutes as above.

apple and almond pudding

serves 6

120 g self-raising flour	3 sharp apples, such as Granny Smith, peeled and thinly sliced
100 g sugar	
1 tsp baking powder	FOR THE TOPPING:
100 g ground almonds	30 g sliced almonds
2 eggs	30 g unrefined golden caster sugar
1 tsp almond extract	
250 g sour cream	

1 Butter the inside of the half-sized roasting tin or a tarte tatin dish or line with Bake-O-Glide.

2 Sift the flour, sugar and baking powder into a bowl, then mix in the ground almonds.

3 Lightly beat the eggs, almond extract and sour cream together and add to the dry ingredients. Do not over-mix.

4 Spoon half the batter over the bottom of the roasting tin, then top with half the apple slices. Spread over the rest of the batter and finish with the remaining apple slices. Scatter over the sliced almonds and caster sugar.

5 Slide the tin on to the fourth set of runners in the ROASTING OVEN and slide in the COLD PLAIN SHELF above. Bake for 20–25 minutes, checking halfway through baking and turning the tin. It should be golden and springy to the touch. For 4-oven Aga owners, bake on the third set of runners in the BAKING OVEN for 35–40 minutes or until a cake tester comes out clean.

6 Cool on a wire rack for 10 minutes. Serve with custard.

Conventional Baking:

Pre-heat the oven to 190ºC/375ºF/gas 5 and bake for 35–40 minutes.

right: rhubarb and orange blossom water clafoutis

stuffed peaches

serves 6

118 g good quality dark chocolate, broken into small pieces

12 very ripe small peaches or 6 large ones, halved and stoned

118 g mascarpone cheese

40 ml honey

59 g slivered almonds (as fresh as possible)

30 ml Amaretto liqueur

1 To melt the chocolate, place in a heatproof bowl on the grid shelf on the floor of the SIMMERING OVEN.

2 Arrange the peaches on a baking tray (slice a little off the bottom to make them sit better if they are very wobbly).

3 Mix together the mascarpone, honey, nuts and Amaretto in a bowl. Spoon some of the mix into each peach cavity.

4 Bake on the third set of runners in the ROASTING OVEN for 10–12 minutes.

5 Remove the bowl of chocolate from the oven and leave at the back of the Aga until needed. Stir it well, making sure all the chocolate has melted.

6 Serve each person with two peach halves, or four if you used small peaches, and drizzle over the melted chocolate.

Conventional Baking:

Pre-heat the oven to 200ºC/400ºF/gas 6 and continue as above.

baked bananas

serves 4–6

8 bananas, peeled and sliced lengthways in half

3 tbsp brown sugar

juice and zest of ½ a lemon

30 ml Malibu

double cream, to serve

1 Lay the bananas in a shallow ovenproof dish and sprinkle over the sugar, zest, juice and 3 tbsp of water.

2 Bake in the ROASTING OVEN for 15 minutes, then pour over the Malibu and transfer to the SIMMERING OVEN for 25–30 minutes or until the bananas are brown and the juice is syrupy. For 4-oven Aga owners, bake the entire recipe in the BAKING OVEN, timings as above. Serve with lots of double cream.

Conventional Baking:

Pre-heat the oven to 200ºC/400ºF/gas 6 and bake the bananas for 15 minutes, then pour in the Malibu, lower the temperature to 180ºC/350ºF/gas 4 and bake for a further 20 minutes.

left: stuffed peaches

raspberry soufflés

serves 4

FOR THE FRUIT BASE:
350 g raspberries
75 g unrefined golden caster sugar
50 ml water

FOR THE CRÈME PÂTISSIÈRE:
25 g cornflour
3 tbsp water
1 egg yolk

FOR THE MERINGUE:
6 egg whites
40 g unrefined golden caster sugar

2 tbsp unsalted butter, for greasing (you won't use all of it)
3 tbsp unrefined golden caster sugar, for coating (again, you won't use all of it)

1 To make the fruit base, put all the ingredients into a saucepan and bring to the boil on the BOILING PLATE. Continue to boil for 2 minutes. Take off the heat, liquidize, strain and then put back into a saucepan.

2 Mix the cornflour and water together in a bowl to make a thin paste.

3 Start whisking the fruit purée on the SIMMERING PLATE and add the cornflour paste little by little, whisking continuously until the mixture thickens.

4 Take off the heat, and, still whisking, add the egg yolk. The consistency should be that of clotted cream. Set aside until ready to use. (Up to this point, the whole process can be made in advance and stored in the fridge for up to 3 days. When you take it out of the fridge, gently warm the fruit mixture so that it comes back to clotted cream consistency.)

5 Grease 4 china ramekins generously with unsalted butter, paying particular attention to the lips of the moulds. Sprinkle a tablespoon of caster sugar into the moulds and swirl it round to dust the inside lightly, making sure the moulds are well coated. Set on to a baking sheet ready to fill.

6 To make the meringue, whisk the egg whites in a mixer, with a scrupulously clean bowl, until stiff. Add the sugar spoonful by spoonful until it is all used up.

7 Fold a large dollop of the meringue into the fruit purée and fold well to loosen the mix. Gently fold in the rest of the meringue until thoroughly blended and with no pockets of 'white' showing.

8 Fill the prepared moulds with the soufflé mixture to the top, then run a clean finger round the lip to form a neat edge. Transfer the soufflés back to the baking sheet, put on the fourth set of runners in the ROASTING OVEN and cook for 8 minutes. Serve directly from the oven.

Conventional Baking:

Pre-heat the oven to 180°C/350°F/gas 4 and cook for 8 minutes.

right: raspberry soufflés

special occasion
baking

celebration fruit cake

for a 15 cm round cake or a 13 cm square cake:

225 g currants	110 g soft unsalted butter
75 g sultanas	110 g soft brown sugar
75 g raisins	110 g plain flour
40 g organic glacé cherries, rinsed, dried and chopped	20 g rice flour
40 g organic candied peel	pinch salt
zest of ½ organic orange	½ tsp mixed spice
zest of ½ organic lemon	2 eggs
½ tbsp treacle	40 g chopped almonds
2 tbsp brandy	

for a 20.5 cm round cake:

450 g currants	225 g soft unsalted butter
175 g sultanas	225 g soft brown sugar
175 g raisins	225 g plain flour
50 g organic glacé cherries, rinsed, dried and chopped	55 g rice flour
50 g organic candied peel	½ tsp salt
zest of 1 organic orange	1 tsp mixed spice
zest of 1 organic lemon	4 eggs
1 tbsp treacle	50 g chopped almonds
3 tbsp brandy	

for a 23 cm round cake or a 20 cm square cake:

575 g currants	275 g soft unsalted butter
225 g sultanas	275 g soft brown sugar
225 g raisins	275 g plain flour
60 g organic glacé cherries, rinsed, dried and chopped	60 g rice flour
60 g organic candied peel	½ tsp salt
zest of 1 organic orange	1 tsp mixed spice
zest of 1 organic lemon	5 eggs
1 tbsp treacle	60 g chopped almonds
4 tbsp brandy	

for a 28 cm round cake or a 25.5 cm square cake:

900 g currants	450 g soft unsalted butter
350 g sultanas	450 g soft brown sugar
350 g raisins	450 g plain flour
100 g organic glacé cherries, rinsed, dried and chopped	65 g rice flour
120 g organic candied peel	½ tsp salt
zest of 2 organic oranges	1½ tsp mixed spice
zest of 2 organic lemons	8 eggs
1½ tbsp treacle	120 g chopped almonds
6 tbsp brandy	

1 Read the special advice on fruit cakes on page 20. The day before making the cake, put the fruit, peel, zests, treacle and brandy in a bowl and mix well. Cover with cling film and leave in a cool place to marinate.

2 Line your tin with Bake-O-Glide if necessary or if the tin is new.

3 When you are ready to make the cake, cream the butter and sugar together until they are pale and fluffy. Sieve the flours, salt and mixed spice together in a bowl. Add the eggs to the butter mix one at a time, alternating with the flour mix until it is all incorporated. If you are doing this with an electric mixer, do it on a very low, gentle speed. If you do it by hand, use a folding motion to mix.

4 Fold in the fruit with all the juices and the almonds. Spoon into the prepared tin.

5 Bake in the ROASTING OVEN for 20 minutes, then transfer to the SIMMERING OVEN for 5–10 hours, depending on your Aga. You can bake it just in the Simmering Oven but it will take longer. The Aga baking time will vary tremendously from Aga to Aga and will take as long as it takes! The great thing about an Aga is that you can open the door and keep on checking.

Conventional Baking:
Pre-heat the oven to 140ºC/275ºF/gas 1. You will need to line the tin and wrap it with a layer of brown paper around the outside and cover the top of the cake with a double layer of greaseproof paper with a small hole cut out for the steam to escape.

The 15 cm round or 13 cm square cake will take 3–3½ hours, but check it after 3 hours.

The 20.5 cm round cake will take 4–5 hours, but check it after 4 hours.

The 23 cm round or 20 cm square cake will take 4–5 hours, but check it after 4 hours.

The 28 cm round or 25.5 cm square cake will take 5–5½ hours, but check it after 5 hours.

marzipan

makes enough to cover a 20 cm round cake

170 g icing sugar, plus extra for kneading
170 g unrefined golden caster sugar
2 organic eggs

340 g ground almonds
2 drops almond extract
1 tsp lemon juice

1 Sift the sugars together in a heatproof bowl, then lightly beat in the eggs.

2 Bring a saucepan of water to the boil on the BOILING PLATE, then move to the SIMMERING PLATE. Place the bowl over the saucepan, making sure the bowl does not touch the water, and whisk the mixture until it is light and creamy and leaves a ribbon trail. Remove the bowl from the heat and set aside to cool completely.

3 When the mixture is cold, add the almonds, almond extract and lemon juice. Dust a worksurface with icing sugar and knead the paste until it is just smooth. Do not over-work the paste. If you do, too much oil will be released. Wrap the marzipan well in cling film and store in a cool, dry place.

simnel cake

serves 6–8

225 g plain flour
1 tsp baking powder
pinch of salt
175 g unsalted butter, softened
174 g soft brown sugar
3 eggs
100 g raisins
175 g currants
100 g sultanas
50 g organic mixed candied peel, chopped

50 g glacé cherries, rinsed, and halved
zest of 1 organic orange
zest of 1 organic lemon
2 tbsp milk
450 g organic marzipan (or see the recipe on page 137)

FOR THE GLAZE:
50 g good quality apricot jam
1 tbsp water

1 Line an 18 cm round cake tin with Bake-O-Glide. If you have a Cake Baker you may want to use it.

2 Sift the flour, baking powder and salt together in a large bowl.

3 Cream the butter and sugar together until pale and fluffy. Add the eggs one at a time to the creamed butter, alternating with the flour until it is all incorporated. Carefully fold in the fruit, candied peel and zest and stir in the milk so everything is evenly incorporated.

4 Roll out one-third of the marzipan to a circle the same size as the cake tin.

5 Spoon half of the cake batter into the tin, cover with the marzipan circle and spoon on the remaining cake mix. Level the top.

6 Slide the COLD PLAIN SHELF on to the fourth set of runners in the ROASTING OVEN. Place the cake on the shelf and bake for 15–20 minutes. Transfer the now hot plain shelf to the SIMMERING OVEN, place the cake on top and bake for 2–5 hours, depending on your oven, until the cake is golden brown and firm in the centre.

7 Cool the cake in the tin on a wire rack. When it is cool, remove from the tin and place on a cake stand.

8 While the cake is cooling, make the apricot glaze. Bring the jam and water to the boil in a saucepan, then pass through a metal sieve. Use it warm.

9 Roll out the remaining marzipan and cut out another circle to fit over the top of the cake. Roll 11 balls from the leftover marzipan scraps (first dip your hands in a little icing sugar to prevent the marzipan sticking to them).

10 Brush a little apricot glaze on to the top of the cake and roll on the marzipan circle. Flute the edges of the marzipan and make a criss-cross pattern with a knife if you wish. Brush a little apricot glaze on to the bottom of each marzipan ball and arrange them in a circle on top of the cake.

Conventional Baking:
Pre-heat the oven to 160ºC/325ºF/gas 3 and bake as above for 2 hours.

panforte

serves 6–8

100 g hazelnuts, coarsely chopped	generous grating of nutmeg
120 g whole blanched almonds	½ tsp ground cinnamon
120 g organic candied orange peel, chopped	½ tsp ground cloves
120 g organic candied lemon peel, chopped	150 g unrefined golden caster sugar
40 g dried figs, coarsely chopped	60 g honey
zest of 1 organic lemon	30 g unsalted butter
70 g rice flour	icing sugar, for dusting

1 Line a 20.5 cm loose bottomed tin with Bake-O-Glide – traditionally this recipe is made in a round shape. Put a piece of rice paper over the Bake-O-Glide on the base of the tin.

2 Spread the hazelnuts and almonds on a shallow baking tray, slide the tray on to the first set of runners in the ROASTING OVEN and roast the nuts until they are golden. Watch them carefully as they will burn very easily.

3 Combine the nuts, candied peels, figs, lemon zest, flour and spices in a large bowl.

4 Melt the sugar, honey and butter in a saucepan on the SIMMERING PLATE, then pour over the dry ingredients and mix really well.

5 Spoon the mixture into the prepared tin, smoothing it down. It is best to do this with your hand – put it into a freezer bag or wet it with a little cold water. Work quickly as the mix will soon stiffen.

6 Put the tin on to the fourth set of runners in the ROASTING OVEN with the COLD PLAIN SHELF on the second set of runners and bake for about 20 minutes. The edges of the cake should be firm but the centre still springy. For 4-oven Aga owners, bake in the BAKING OVEN for 30–35 minutes using the COLD PLAIN SHELF halfway through baking if necessary.

7 Cool in the tin on a wire rack – the panforte will harden as it cools. When the cake is completely cold, remove it from the tin, then dust it generously with icing sugar and store in an airtight tin. It will keep for months if stored correctly.

Conventional Baking:
Pre-heat the oven to 180ºC/350ºF/gas 4 and bake for 30–40 minutes.

bread sticks

To ring the changes, you can sprinkle the bread sticks with different seeds such as poppy, nigella or fennel, or add spices to the basic dough mix. I like to add a good pinch of saffron to the liquid mix to give a superb flavour and colour to the sticks, or add cayenne and paprika for a real kick. Add the dry spices to the dry mix.

makes about 32 sticks, depending on length

30 ml olive oil, plus extra for greasing	380 g strong flour
11 ml honey	2 tsp sea salt
220 ml warm water	10 g Parmesan cheese, finely grated
20 g dry yeast	

1 Combine all the liquid ingredients together in a bowl and mix well.

2 Mix all the dry ingredients together in a large bowl, then slowly add the wet to the dry and combine well until it is all incorporated into a dough. I usually do this in my Kitchen Aid using the dough hook attachment, but you can do it by hand.

3 Knead the dough for about 8 minutes or until you have a smooth and elastic dough.

4 Grease the inside of a large bowl with olive oil and pop the dough in it to prove. Cover with a tea towel and leave next to the Aga for 45–60 minutes until doubled in size.

5 When the dough has risen, divide it into four, then divide each four into eight long thin sticks. Do this in batches and lay the sticks on a baking sheet about 3 cm apart. Cover the first batch with the tea towel and proceed with the second batch. When you have finished with the second batch, brush the first batch with olive oil and sprinkle over some salt.

6 Slide the tray on to the floor of the ROASTING OVEN and bake for 10–12 minutes. Repeat until all the dough is used up.

Conventional Baking:
Pre-heat the oven to 200ºC/400ºF/gas 6 and bake for 10–12 minutes.

right: bread sticks

cheese sticks

makes about 18–20, depending how you cut them

60 g plain flour	25 g ground almonds
½ tsp baking powder	100 g strong Cheddar cheese, grated
½ tsp powdered mustard	salt and pepper
55 g butter	1 egg yolk
30 g fine breadcrumbs	1 tbsp water

1 Line a shallow baking tray with Bake-O-Glide.

2 Sift the flour, baking powder and mustard together in a large bowl and rub in the butter.

3 Rub in the breadcrumbs, almonds and cheese and mix well. Season. Beat the yolk with the water and stir into the dry mixture to form a dough, but take care not to over-work it.

4 Roll out the dough on a floured surface to a thickness of 5 mm and cut into sticks. The size depends on personal preference – the smaller and thinner, the shorter the baking time.

5 Transfer the sticks to the baking tray and bake on the second set of runners in the ROASTING OVEN for 5–8 minutes. Turn the baking tray around halfway through the baking time and turn the sticks over when they are golden on top – you will have to watch them carefully.

6 Cool on a wire rack and serve with drinks.

Conventional Baking:

Pre-heat the oven to 200ºC/400ºF/gas 6 and bake for 8–10 minutes.

olive, orange and rosemary biscotti

Biscotti are the perfect party food because you can make them ahead of time, and the dough also freezes well. Once the dough is formed into logs, freeze it like cookie dough. When you are ready to use it, defrost thoroughly and continue with the recipe. Once baked, the biscotti will keep in an airtight tin for up to a week.

makes about 18, depending how thick you slice them

270 g self-raising flour
2 tsp baking powder
black pepper
200 g stoned black Kalamata olives in olive oil, halved
zest of 1 organic orange (make the zests long and thin)
1 tbsp freshly chopped rosemary

3 eggs
olive oil from the olives

FOR THE EGG WASH:
beaten egg or milk
sea salt

1 Sieve the flour and baking powder into a large bowl. Add the pepper, olives, zest and rosemary and mix well. Beat the eggs with 2 tbsp of the olive oil and then pour them into the dry ingredients and mix well – you can do this in an electric mixer using the paddle attachment. The dough will be very soft and slightly wet.

2 Turn out the soft dough on to a floured surface and shape into a flattish loaf. Place on a baking sheet lined with Bake-O-Glide and brush lightly with a little beaten egg or milk and sprinkle with sea salt.

3 Slide the baking tray on to the fourth set of runners in the ROASTING OVEN with the COLD PLAIN SHELF above and bake for 20–30 minutes or until golden. For 4-oven Aga owners, bake in the BAKING OVEN for 25–35 minutes. Remove the loaf from the oven and cool on a wire rack. Set the lined baking tray aside.

4 When it is cool, slice the loaf on the diagonal 2.5 cm thick. Lay the slices on the lined baking tray and bake in the SIMMERING OVEN for about 20 minutes or until the biscotti are crisp. Cool the biscotti on a wire rack and store in an airtight tin.

Conventional Baking:
Pre-heat the oven to 200ºC/400ºF/gas 6 and bake for 20–30 minutes, then bake the biscotti slices for another 20 minutes.

rosemary and dijon gougères

makes about 45 – perfect for a party!

110 ml milk	1 tbsp Dijon mustard
110 ml water	pinch of cayenne pepper
50 g butter	2 tsp chopped rosemary leaves
pinch of salt	black pepper
100 g plain flour	
3 eggs	FOR THE GLAZE
50 g Gruyère cheese, grated	1 egg yolk, mixed with 1 tsp water
	sea salt

1 Line a shallow baking tray with Bake-O-Glide.

2 Put the milk, water, butter and salt into a saucepan and bring it to the boil on the SIMMERING PLATE. Remove it from the heat and quickly add in the flour, stirring vigorously with a wooden spoon until well combined. Put the pan back on the SIMMERING PLATE and stir for about 1 minute or until the mix comes away from the sides of the pan.

3 Tip the mix into a bowl and, using an electric hand whisk, beat in the eggs one at a time until combined. Add the cheese, mustard, cayenne and rosemary and season to taste with salt and pepper. Mix well.

4 Drop teaspoonfuls of the mix on to the prepared tray and brush each mound with a little of the egg glaze.

Sprinkle with a little sea salt and a rosemary leaf if you have any left over.

5 Slide the tray on to the fourth set of runners in the ROASTING OVEN and bake for 10 minutes, then slide the COLD PLAIN SHELF on to the second set of runners and bake for a further 10–12 minutes or until puffed up and golden. For 4-oven Aga owners, move them to the BAKING OVEN after the first 10 minutes of baking time. Serve straight away!

Conventional Baking:

Pre-heat oven to 200ºC/400ºF/gas 6 and bake for 10 minutes, then turn the oven down to 190ºC/375ºF/gas 5 and bake for a further 15 minutes.

christmas tart

serves 6

1 small quantity sweet pastry (see page 70)

FOR THE FILLING:
120 g unsalted butter
120 g icing sugar
2 large eggs

2 tbsp double cream
120 g ground almonds
1 tsp pure almond extract
230 g mincemeat
60 g flaked almonds

1 Line a 23 cm loose bottomed tart tin with sweet pastry and chill in the fridge.

2 Cream the butter and sugar together in a bowl, then add the eggs and cream and mix well. Fold in the ground almonds and almond extract.

3 Spread a thin layer of mincemeat over the base of the pastry and spoon the almond mix on top. Scatter over the flaked almonds.

4 Bake the tart on the floor of the ROASTING OVEN for 25 minutes or until firm in the centre and golden on top. Slide the COLD PLAIN SHELF on the third set of runners after 10 minutes if browning too quickly.

Conventional Baking:

Pre-heat the oven to 190ºC/275ºF/gas 5 and blind-bake the pastry case for 10–15 minutes. Leave to cool, then add the filling and bake at 190ºC/275ºF/gas 5 for 25 minutes.

chocolate chip cookies for the christmas tree

Feel free to halve the quantities if you just want to make a batch of cookies. Don't forget you can make this dough up to one month before cooking; freeze in logs wrapped in greaseproof paper. If you wish, you can also make star-shaped cookies by pressing the dough into a baking tray to a thickness of 2 cm, refrigerating for 1 hour and then cutting out with a star-shaped cookie cutter.

makes 25–30 cookies

450 g unsalted butter, softened
700 g soft unrefined brown sugar
200 g unrefined granulated sugar
4 large eggs
seeds from one vanilla pod

930 g plain flour
½ tsp salt
2 tsp baking powder
450 g plain chocolate chips

1 Cream the butter and sugars together until smooth and fluffy. Add the eggs one at a time and scrape in the vanilla seeds.

2 Put the flour, salt and baking powder into a sieve and sift into the butter mix. Fold to combine thoroughly, then add the chocolate chips.

3 Drop 2 tablespoons of the dough one of top of the other on a baking sheet. Repeat to use up all the dough, spacing the cookies about 5 cm apart. Bake for 8 minutes on the fourth set of runners in the ROASTING OVEN with the COLD PLAIN SHELF on the second set of runners. Cook in batches and remove to a wire rack.

4 While they are still hot, make a hole one third of the way down the cookie with a clean, round pen top. Let the cookies cool completely. String a pretty ribbon through and tie in a loop so that you can hang them on the Christmas tree.

Conventional Baking:
Pre-heat the oven to 190ºC/375ºF/gas 5 and bake the cookies as above.

right: chocolate chip cookies for the christmas tree

gingerbread house

You will need to make two batches of this gingerbread dough to make a house of the size given on the templates on page 151, but you can of course make a house of any shape and size you wish.

150 g lard	3 tsp ground ginger
650 g plain flour	2 tsp ground cinnamon
1 tsp baking soda	½ tsp ground cloves
1 tsp salt	250 ml treacle
1 tsp fresh nutmeg, grated	145 g unrefined golden caster sugar

1 Gently melt the lard in a saucepan on the SIMMERING PLATE.

2 Sift the flour, baking soda, salt and spices together into a large bowl.

3 When the lard has melted, stir in the treacle and sugar and mix well. Take care as the mixture will be hot. Pour the wet mix into the dry and stir it well. It will come together to form a dough. Turn it out on to a clean surface and shape into a large flattish disc. Wrap the dough in cling film and leave to rest in the refrigerator for 30 minutes. Bring the dough to room temperature before rolling out.

4 Copy the templates from page 151.

5 When you are ready to bake the gingerbread, line large flat baking trays (preferably without a lip) with Bake-O-Glide and roll the dough directly on the lined tray to a thickness of about 1 cm. Place the templates for the front and back walls on the raw dough and cut out the shapes with a sharp knife, removing the excess dough. Cut out any windows and doors at this stage. Make up a second batch of gingerbread dough and repeat the process to make the side walls and roof panels of the house.

6 Bake the gingerbread on the fourth set of runners in the ROASTING OVEN with the COLD PLAIN SHELF directly above it for 15 minutes, then turn the baking tray and continue baking for another 15 minutes. (This is where having several cold plain shelves comes in handy. To cool quickly, run cold water over the hot shelf. I have two large flat baking trays and can bake two sides of a house at a time, placing one baking tray on the fourth set of runners and one on the third set with the cold plain shelf directly above. When I turn the gingerbread, I also swap them on the runners.)

7 Remove the baking trays to wire cooling racks and cool the gingerbread completely before assembling (see page 150). It is a good idea to make the gingerbread the day before decorating and assembling.

Conventional Baking:

Pre-heat the oven to 190°C/375°F/gas 5 and bake as above, turning the trays halfway through baking.

right: gingerbread house

meringue for gluing and decorating

This meringue mix will be the glue for sticking together the sides and roof of the house as well as for decorating. If possible, use an electric mixer.

8 large egg whites
300 g white caster sugar

pinch of cream of tartar

1 Put a saucepan of water on the SIMMERING PLATE and let the water come up to a simmer.

2 Place the egg whites, sugar and cream of tartar into a large bowl over the simmering water (the bowl of the electric mixer would be best). Whisk until the sugar has dissolved and the whites are warm. Test with your fingers. This will take about 2–3 minutes.

3 Transfer the bowl to the mixer and, starting on the lowest speed, start to whisk the meringue, gradually increasing the speed to high until the meringue is cool, stiff and glossy. This will take about 10 minutes. You may need to make a few batches depending on the size of your house. Use immediately.

Assembling the house

You will need someone to help you construct the house. Sides will need to be held together so choose someone with a lot of patience! The template is only a guide – this is your chance to build the house of your dreams!

1 Assemble the house on a large tray that is easy to move. It is best to decide where the house will be displayed before you start as this may determine the size. Use the meringue icing as glue and spread the edges of the sides, front, back and roof liberally. I sometimes use straight pins stuck into the corners to help hold the house together until it dries. Don't forget to pull them out before displaying and eating!

2 The house should be covered in lots of icicles and snow drifts so it doesn't matter if the icing oozes through. Be as decorative with the façade as you like using different piping bag tips – it is suppose to look like a winter wonderland. Dust with icing sugar to give that 'just snowed' look. Fresh greenery around the bottom of the house looks good too. You can add embellishments if you like.

3 I use gelatine leaves for the window 'glass' as they have a criss-cross pattern on them resembling leaded windows. Use the icing to hold them place around the inside of the façade. Do this before putting the house together. If you can find tiny battery-operated fairy lights, put them inside the house. Decide which door or window to leave ajar for switching them on and off. You can also use a votive candle under supervision.

TEMPLATES FOR THE GINGERBREAD HOUSE

Enlarge these templates to 200% on a photocopier to make the cake shown in the photograph

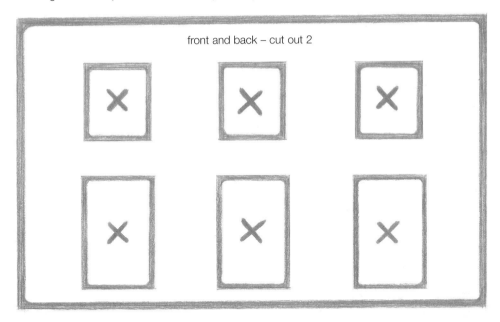

front and back – cut out 2

X cut out for windows and door

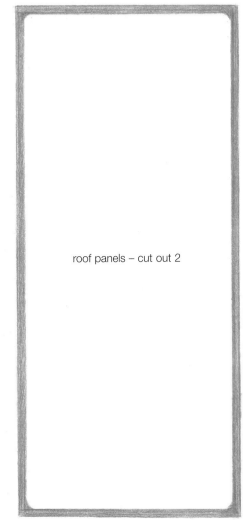

roof panels – cut out 2

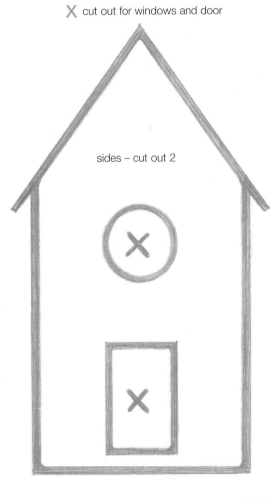

sides – cut out 2

**mummy's little
helpers**

yo yo biscuits

makes about 18 medium-sized biscuits

60 g icing sugar	60 g custard powder
170 g butter	candy-coated chocolate buttons, to decorate
175 g self-raising flour	

1 Line a shallow baking tray with Bake-O-Glide.

2 Cream the icing sugar and butter together. Stir in the flour and custard powder. Roll the mixture into balls and place on the baking tray. Flatten each ball with a fork and push in a chocolate button.

3 Bake the biscuits on the fourth set of runners in the ROASTING OVEN with the COLD PLAIN SHELF above for 8–10 minutes or until done. Do not over-bake – the biscuits should be yellow, not brown. Cool them on a wire rack.

Conventional Baking:
Pre-heat the oven to 150°C/300°F/gas 2 and bake for 15–18 minutes or until done.

gwen's cornflake cakes

This is my mother-in-law's recipe and I know the powdered milk sounds strange but I can assure you it is very necessary. It gives a sort of fudgyness to these very adult cornflake cakes. In my mother-in-law's day everything was weighed in ounces so it was all four of everything!

makes about 12

125 g butter	4 tbsp powdered baby milk
4 tbsp golden syrup	125 g cornflakes
4 tbsp cocoa powder	

1 Lay out paper cake cases on a baking tray or a large flat plate.

2 Gently melt the butter and golden syrup in a saucepan on the SIMMERING PLATE, then stir in the cocoa powder and powdered baby milk until the mixture is smooth.

3 Add the cornflakes and stir gently to avoid breaking them up. Spoon the mixture into the paper cases and refrigerate until firm.

Conventional Baking:
Melt on a hob.

rice crispy cakes

makes about 10

60 g unsalted butter
250 g marshmallows

1 tsp vanilla extract
1–2 teacups rice crispies

1 Melt the butter and marshmallows in a large saucepan on the SIMMERING PLATE. Add the vanilla extract and stir in the rice crispies. Take care not to crush them too much.

2 Lay out paper cases on a baking tray or large plate and spoon some of the mix into each case. Leave to cool in the fridge.

Conventional Baking:
Melt the butter and marshmallows on the hob.

peanut butter cupcakes

makes 12 large cupcakes

225 g unsalted butter or margarine, very soft
200 g unrefined golden caster sugar
275 g self-raising flour
2 tsp baking powder
4 large eggs
4 tbsp milk
125 g peanut butter

FOR THE PEANUT BUTTER CREAM ICING:
3 large egg whites
155 g unrefined golden caster sugar
375 g peanut butter

1 Line a muffin tin with paper cake cases and set aside.

2 Cream the butter and sugar together. Sieve the flour and baking powder into a bowl. Add the eggs to the sugar and butter one at a time, alternating with the flour until all combined. Beat in the milk and peanut butter.

3 Fill the cupcake cases half-full and level off the tops. Bake on the fourth set of runners in the ROASTING OVEN for 20 minutes, checking halfway through and turning the tray if necessary. They are done when they spring back when gently pressed on top.

4 Remove from tin and cool on a wire rack.

5 To make the icing, place the egg whites and sugar in a large heatproof bowl. Set the bowl over a pot of simmering water, creating a bain marie, and whisk the sugar and egg whites until the sugar has dissolved.

6 When ready take the bowl off the heat and use an electric whisk to whisk the mix until it starts to form soft peaks. Add the peanut butter little by little until it is all combined. Chill until it becomes stiff but still spreadable, then use to ice the cupcakes

Conventional Baking:
Pre-heat the oven to 200ºC/400ºF/gas 6 and bake for 20 minutes, as above. Make the icing on the hob.

peter rabbit cake

serves 10–12

700 g self-raising flour

1 tbsp baking powder

1 tsp salt

1 tbsp ground cinnamon

700 g unrefined golden caster sugar

350 ml grapeseed oil

4 large eggs, lightly beaten

1 tbsp vanilla extract

350 g chopped walnuts

350 g desiccated coconut

350 g carrots, cooked and puréed

175 g crushed pineapple

FOR THE ICING:

118 g unsalted butter, softened

300 g pack cream cheese

700 g icing sugar

1 tsp vanilla extract

FOR THE DECORATION:

400 g chocolate cookies, cream centres removed and the biscuits crushed very finely

20–30 marzipan vegetables (either make your own from coloured marzipan or buy from cake decorating shops)

1 Grease the large roasting tin and line with Bake-O-Glide.

2 Sift the flour, baking powder, salt and cinnamon into the bowl of an electric mixer, then add the rest of the cake ingredients and mix well.

3 Pour into the tin and bake on the fourth set of runners in the ROASTING OVEN with the COLD PLAIN SHELF on the second set of runners for 40–50 minutes or until the sides pull away from the tin and a skewer comes out clean. For 4-oven Aga owners, use the BAKING OVEN and bake for 45–50 minutes. Cool on a wire rack until completely cold.

4 To make the icing, using an electric beater, beat the butter and cream cheese together until smooth. Slowly add the icing sugar and vanilla extract until it is lump-free and very smooth. Ice the cake with the cream cheese icing.

5 To decorate, sprinkle the cookie 'dirt' on the icing and carefully arrange the marzipan fruits on top. If you wish, you can 'build' a fence with extra marzipan.

Conventional Baking:

Pre-heat the oven to 190°C/375°F/gas 5 and bake for 50–60 minutes.

flapjack firelighters

makes about 10

240 g unsalted butter

240 g demerara sugar

2 tbsp golden syrup

280 g rolled oats or muesli

1 Line a shallow baking tray with Bake-O-Glide.

2 Melt the butter, sugar and syrup in a small saucepan on the SIMMERING PLATE. Stir in the oats or muesli and press into the baking tray.

3 Slide on to the fourth set of runners in the ROASTING OVEN and bake for 10 minutes or until golden. For 4-oven Aga owners, slide the tin on to the third set of runners in the BAKING OVEN and bake for 15 minutes.

4 Remove from the oven, mark into squares or bars and cool on a wire rack. Store in an airtight tin.

Conventional Baking:

Pre-heat the oven to 190°C/375°F/gas 5 and bake for 10–15 minutes or until golden.

above: peter rabbit cake

date goodies

makes about 24

250 g butter	2 packets ginger biscuits, crushed
200 g chopped dates	2 eggs, beaten
160 g unrefined golden caster sugar	250 g desiccated coconut, plus more for coating
2 tsp vanilla extract	

1 Put the butter, dates and sugar into a saucepan and bring up to the boil on the BOILING PLATE.

2 Take off the heat and stir in the vanilla extract, biscuits and eggs. Sprinkle half the desiccated coconut over the bottom of a small shallow tin, then press the date mix into the tin, sprinkling the remaining coconut over the top.

3 Let the goodies cool, then cut into small squares and roll in more coconut. These will keep for about 1 week in an airtight tin.

Conventional Baking:

Melt the butter and date mixture on the hob.

index

Amy Willcock's own range of cookware called *Rangeware* is produced by *Mermaid*.

For your nearest stockist, please telephone 0121 554 2001.

www.mermaidcookware.com